# SAY TO THE DARKNESS, WE BEG TO DIFFER

## Mary Jo Leddy

LESTER
&ORPEN
DENNYS

FIRST EDITION

**Canadian Cataloguing in Publication Data**
Leddy, Mary Joanna, 1946-
   Say to the darkness, we beg to differ
ISBN   0-88619-346-X

1.   Church and social problems - Catholic Church.
I.   Title.

HN37.C3L43   1990    261.8    C90-094484-6


The Publisher wishes to acknowledge the assistance of the Ontario Arts Council.

Cover design by Stephen Latimer

Printed and bound in Canada

Lester & Orpen Dennys Limited
78 Sullivan Street
Toronto, Canada M5T 1C1

When we light
a candle at midnight
we say to the darkness
we beg to differ.

*Graffiti on Queen St. West wall*

*For my co-workers at* Catholic New Times
*and my friends of New Year's Eve,*
*and for Basya Hunter*

# Acknowledgements

Although this entire book is an acknowledgement of those who have contributed to the shape of my life and my writing, I want to express my gratitude to those who helped to make this specific volume possible.

My agent, Lee Davis Creal (Lucinda Vardey Agency), convinced me that such a project was not only worthwhile but also possible. Louise Dennys and Malcolm Lester welcomed the initial idea for this book and trusted me to give it form and substance.

Several people offered me the space in which to gather up my reflections: the Genesis Community, Mary McCann IHM and Rebecca McKenna CND in Toronto; the Madonna House Community in Gravelbourg, Saskatchewan.

Lauretta Santarossa was an enthusiastic supporter of this entire project. Carol Rittner RSM generously donated the computer which made the production of this manuscript so much more enjoyable.

Finally, I want to thank Gena Gorrell, senior editor at Lester & Orpen Dennys, for her invaluable assistance in preparing the final copy for production.

# CONTENTS

# Introduction

Only some of my dreams are luminous. There is a young girl playing in white light snow. She lifts her face and is washed by the falling brightness. Then she joins hands and dances with other children through the snow. Their circle widens and widens until....

The alarm sounds and I open my eyes. It is grey. It is now.

There are nightmares too. I am a child with a yellow star on my forehead watching the smoke darken the sky. I am a child wandering through a barrio looking for my brothers and sisters who were taken away by the men in black boots. I am a child who is not white....

And then the alarm sounds. It is grey. It is here.

These dreams and nightmares have grown up inside me for the last fifteen years. They have drawn and shadowed me over the course of this time. I cannot abandon the children of my nightmares without denying the children of my dreams.

1

In 1975 a small group of us began to talk about starting an alternative Catholic newspaper in Canada. It was our not-so-humble opinion that the official church publication (the conservative *Catholic Register*) was proving woefully inadequate in its coverage of more promising contemporary developments.

Unlike many other earnest discussions I was engaged in at the time, this one began to go somewhere. To this day I am amazed that what ensued was the audacious decision to initiate the publication of *Catholic New Times*. This was a decision with consequences I never could have foreseen.

Much to my surprise, *Catholic New Times* not only survived but grew. In the process of its development, it has been praised lavishly and criticized vehemently. I leave it to someone more objective to tell the story of this newspaper and to assess its value and significance. But this much I can say for sure: I am grateful for what the paper has become because of who I have become through my association with it.

Almost by default (everyone else was "too busy") I found myself with the responsibility for editing *Catholic New Times*. It became a weight in my life. By this I mean more than the fact that it was often a worrisome burden. It also gave weight to my life, taught me how to weigh my life.

Before 1975, there were ways in which mine was a rather floating existence — although not obviously so. After all, I had made the seemingly weighty decision to make a commitment within a religious community; and I had chosen to study something so apparently substantial as philosophy. Yet my sense of vocation was vague and my questions were quite academic: i.e., they didn't really demand answers. I could easily have floated off, a make-believe person in a make-believe world.

As I began to write for *Catholic New Times*, and then for other publications such as the *Toronto Star*, I was forced to define myself publicly—where I stood, with whom, and why. The process was exciting and occasionally disconcerting. I was drawn into issues and events, in Canada and elsewhere, that commanded my attention and summoned my response. I was pulled further into the reality of the Roman Catholic church, a reality which was both worse and better than I ever could have imagined.

The weighty decisions I was sometimes faced with had everything to do with the gravity of the times. These past fifteen years, in the church and in the world, have been momentous. This has been a period in which hope and fear have mingled, faith and doubt have been intertwined, violence and oppression have grown along with the thirst for peace and liberation. I could have saved myself a good deal of grief by staying outside all this—but only at the cost of my own soul.

My own soul. The point of my being. For a long time, I refused to write publicly about my own personal experience. I told myself (and others) that this would be a form of self-indulgence. It would have been more honest to say that I preferred the protection afforded by objective reporting and issue-oriented opinion pieces. This style of writing did enable me to maintain a certain consistency of position. Given the intermittent pressure on me to change my views, such consistency was sometimes an important achievement.

Nevertheless, I remained more tentative and perhaps more truthful in my own soul. I had more doubts about the church, about the left, about myself, than I ever acknowledged in print. Through this soul-searching I always found myself grounded, once again, in grace. I reserved such reflections for my journal, where I tried to draw a fine line between my public and more personal life. The line, in fact, was always being crossed. Now I sense that the line which used to serve as a protective boundary has become an unnecessary barrier in the telling of a longer and deeper story that is at once more truthful and more hopeful.

The structure of this book reflects the dynamic of one person's public and private reflections on a significant period in the church and in this culture. Most of my published writings were written in the heat of the moment, under the pressure of a deadline or because of the urgency of a situation. The journal entries simply happened whenever they did. There was only one day a year when I committed myself to writing an entry, and that was New Year's Day.

The night before was held as sacred by a group of eight of us who had become friends through the survival course called graduate school. We were all baby-boomers and Catholics in a conscious sort of way: younger priests, sisters, and lay people who were as uncomfortable in the institutional church as we were in the academic establishment. In the early seventies we decided to set aside New Year's Eve to share our experiences of the year that had passed and our hopes for the year to come. There was always lots of fine food and wine, raucous laughter, and moments of more serious conversation.

As the years flew by, many of the original group left Toronto for other places in Canada, the United States, and elsewhere. Yet some would always return for the gathering on New Year's Eve, often bringing with them family or new friends. We helped each other struggle through various crises and provided one another with many an excuse to celebrate.

I have included these New Year's reflections in this book because they suggest how my story relates to the story of a whole generation in the church. We were those whose first real commitments took shape at a time when there was every reason to be optimistic about the future of our church and our culture, and our place in both. The Second Vatican Council had thrown open the door of the church to the modern world, and we were ready, willing, and able to stride confidently into that world. We were a generation waiting for a call. And we were called. People like John Kennedy and Pierre Elliott Trudeau asked for all we had to give in the building of a more just society. We were the future, or so we were told. So we believed.

As the eighties wore on, there was reason to doubt that future. It seemed greyer, darker, more distant than ever. And worse: we were faced with the darkness not only around us but within us as well. Now we had reason to wonder about the light.

This book is written in response to a summons, as new as it is old, to say something about the darkness and the light. Which do we believe carries more weight in the world? The evidence of history does not suggest an obvious answer. And so much hangs in the balance. In the end, I believe this is a question of faith to which we can only respond with our lives: which shall prevail — the darkness or the light? Only our lives give weight to our words.

In the four major sections of this book, I have delineated the shifts that have taken place in the light-dark world of my own life over the past fifteen years. I have selected those published articles which relate, directly or indirectly, to the underlying question that animates this book. These selections have been edited to make them more comprehensible. In the journal entries I have altered the names and identifiable characteristics of those who had no intention, at the time, of relating to me as a journalist. This seemed appropriate and fair.*

As I look over all of this material there is much more that I am tempted to rewrite. However, I know that polishing to perfection sometimes results in more lustre than light. I am also aware that life, my life or anyone else's, is not as sectioned off as the outlines of this book seem to indicate. While I can speak of a predominant perspective of certain periods of my life, I cannot deny the seemingly inconsistent experiences in those periods that also cry out to be acknowledged. Eventually I began to see that those apparent inconsistencies carried within them their own revelation.

The first section of this book relates to the early years of *Catholic New Times* — 1975 to 1978 — an exuberantly optimistic time, a moment of creation which seemed to encompass the darkness which I, as a woman, was already experiencing in the institutional church. It was also the time when I was surprised by love. I looked on *the bright side of things*.

This brightness seemed to disappear for ever during the two-year period from 1978 to 1980, when I took time off the newspaper to finish my doctoral dissertation on the Holocaust. For me this was *the dead of night*. I was with the dead of night. I wrote almost nothing for publication during those two years. My dissertation was really a collection of little scratches written in the dark, notes to remind myself about what not to forget. I caught sight of radical evil. I saw its shape, its deformed shape, in the twentieth century. This glimpse was brief enough to leave me with my sight, long enough to make me see through illusions and empty rhetoric about the light.

---

* Most of these articles are entirely mine. However, I have indicated those articles which reflect the consensus of a group, i.e. editorials. In these cases, I usually wrote the first draft and revised it after the discussion in the editorial committee.

I emerged from this brief acquaintance with the dead of night with *a certain clarity*. I refused to dwell in the grey zone of moral neutrality. I renounced the role of a bystander. I resisted silence as a dangerous luxury.

This shift coincided with an outpouring of articles, from 1980 to 1984, which were passionate statements about the importance of resisting darkness in the church and in the world. During this time the build-up of nuclear arms reached a crisis point, and I became actively involved in the peace movement, convinced that the moral middle ground had disappeared on this issue. This involvement put me in touch with several people, in Canada and elsewhere, who were saying to the darkness, "We beg to differ." Many of my stories from this time are portraits of these people, persistent lights in the midst of pervasive darkness.

In the following years, from 1984 to 1990, I was less intimately involved with the day-to-day operations of *Catholic New Times*. This change was initially due to my election to assume responsibility for leadership of my own community in North America. I spent many hours listening to the joys and sufferings of individuals and became more attentive to how each person is a whole world in herself. And I began to recognize the pervasive darkness and persistent light that existed within myself as well. The accumulation of so many hours spent with such seemingly small stories resulted in an important qualification: I learned that, although there are times when greyness must be resisted, there are also times when its reality must be respected. I discovered, in the midst of these many moments, *a modicum of light*. I wrote less frequently, of necessity and by choice. Although I could no longer believe silence was golden, I sometimes trusted that there was a faint glimmer to be mined from its depths.

This was also a time of profound spiritual awakening.

I met a wise old woman who had been to the other side of darkness and had returned with dreams—oh, such dreams! She had almost died. She told me that it was all light on the other side of this most ultimate darkness. And when she did finally breathe her last, I saw her defer to this light as she died. She had given the darkness its due but she would not let it have the last word. Her final words welled up from some pool of light within her. As I watched her go, I felt two ancient hands reach out for the child of my dreams and the child of my nightmares. Holding each by the hand, she walked between them as they went together down the long road ahead.

And so each day I am awakened by a sound. Sometimes it is an alarm signalling that now is the moment to differ from the darkness. At other times it is a bell ringing out that now is the hour to defer to the light.

# I

*The Bright Side of Things*

*New Year's Day, 1976*
Good to be together: Ann, Mark, Jim, Isabel, Luigi, and Bill.

Mostly we're restless. Like caged lions. The university seems less and less believable as a place to spend all or part of one's life. Maybe we came here to learn, but the most important things we're learning from each other. The course work is done but we're drifting in and out of any real work on our dissertations. Feel like we're jumping through academic hoops when other people are putting their lives on the line. I told the others that the university is no longer the place where the most significant thinking is taking place. Mark said I should quit the program if I really believed that. "Let's burn our student cards!" Jim shouted. I was saved from taking up Mark's challenge by a loud cheer and another toast to "freedom".

The war in Nam is over now so we can joke about burning cards. Another toast, to the end of the war. Ann,

Jim, Mark, and Isabel (Americans all) toasted again "to the end of the nightmare we grew up with."

It's over and it's not over. Jim talked about a friend, quadriplegic, he had visited in a veterans' hospital over the holidays. Some of my classmates (draft dodgers), the brightest and the best, are now over at the Clarke Institute of Psychiatry. A month ago they found Vince in a snow-drift, the morning after the night before — stoned out of his mind. Both hands and feet had to be amputated.

It's not over and yet it is over. We knew what we were against and now we have to find out what we're for.

We're all into hobbies (me, plants). In the evenings, Bill is playing lead guitar for a folk group. Ann has taken up the flute, and Isabel knitting. Mark and Jim are brewing beer in the basement of their community house. Not a very priestly activity! The least they could do is make mass wine! Luigi spends his mornings at a subway station passing out flyers about the California Grape Boycott. Anything to escape the library.

I brought the others up to date on the meetings we've been having about possibly starting an alternative news-paper. We've been meeting for a couple of months — gal-vanized by the shocking editorials in the *Catholic Register* supporting apartheid. Still not sure we can make this paper happen but want to. None of us knows anything about publishing. We can learn.

*October 1976*
This is the point of no return. We know we don't know enough to plan any further. We can only begin, begin now and discover what needs to be done as we go along. We've called the paper *Catholic New Times*. Advance issue (December 2) to coincide with the anniversary of the death of Thomas Merton. We've organized ourselves into a collective working group. I'm to be editor for now — it

should take about a day a week, which will allow me to continue my chaplaincy work. The first issue will be flogged at all the Catholic gatherings. We should know soon whether it can fly. Of course we are unrealistic — that's what feels so wonderful, after years of being forced to think in cramped and correct little ways.

Decided to start small instead of big and glossy. Religious communities (mostly the women's communities) have given us some start-up money but it won't carry us very far unless we can get enough subscriptions. We'll have about nine months before we know whether the paper is born or stillborn. My first challenge is to learn how to typeset. And then I have to do something about my spelling.

Last big question was whether or not to ask the archbishop for permission. Decided not to. We're assuming we all have an obligation to preach the good news.

OUR COMMITMENT AND HOPE
(Editorial, *Catholic New Times* [CNT], Dec. 2, 1976)

These are good times.
These are hard times.
These are our times
and, in the end,
God's time.

Over ten years ago the Vatican Council articulated a genuinely new understanding of the church and its relationship to the world. The vision it presented was rooted in the past and yet it pointed to a radically different future. During the sixties and the early seventies there was a time of real ferment in the church. It was a time of change, a time of hope and of fear.

Where do we go from here? There are many different answers to that question in the church today. Some feel that we must go back if we are to go anywhere at all. Others, who courageously put on the sandals of pilgrims, have stopped at different oases in the desert, tired of the heat of the day. Many look on the years after Vatican II as a vibrant but somewhat reckless time that must now be given some form of stability if the deeper values are not to be lost in the rush and flow of uncritical change. Then too, there are those who are frantically looking for another cause now that the "novelty" of Vatican II has worn off.

Is the time of Vatican II drawing to a close or is it just beginning? *Catholic New Times* is a collective effort involving people who could so easily be described by the traditional categories: men and women; young and old; priests, sisters, and laity. What is not so easy to describe is the common conviction we share which eludes all our easy categories. We believe something new is coming to birth. It is not that we are by nature optimistic. It is not that it is so obviously happening in us. It is simply that we see something new happening in the lives of so many people. The strength of this new life breaks through previous definitions and includes the most diverse kinds of people and movements. It is present, for example, in the serious explorations of scholars, in the struggle for justice, in the search for deeper human relationships, in the creativity of catechists, in the renewal of religious life, in the praise of pentecostals, in the leadership of some bishops, in the heartfelt wisdom of the retarded, in the quiet fidelity of a pastor in the north, in the laughter of a child and the silent courage of an old woman in the face of death. This is the church that is in the process of reimagining itself.

We have taken no rigid position on the left, right, or centre of the church. However, we will speak as truthfully as we can on issues as they present themselves. Our primary commitment is to listen to the experience of people in our times, to report on it and to reflect on this in the light of the scriptures. We can do no more. We can do no less.

*Catholic New Times* can only begin from where we are at this time and in this place. We begin as Catholics, Canadians, and citizens of Toronto. This is merely a realistic beginning. It does not limit the end we have in sight.

We begin from a deep commitment to the church which is not uncritical. From this common ground we want to reach out to other religious people who work and wait for the reign of God in the world.

We begin as Canadians concerned with the situation of our country. Yet we are aware of the inescapable fact that we are connected in many ways with the lives of people throughout the world. Whether these connections are creative or destructive is the significant issue in the struggle for justice today.

We begin in Toronto — the centre of so much that is both good and bad in our country. Toronto is Bay Street. It is also an exciting experiment in multiculturalism, a church of immigrants, and a place of resistance to the unbridled power of corporate development. In Toronto, the capital of consumerism, we all live behind a "plastic curtain". However, we believe that freedom cannot be found in moving to another place, to new frontiers to the west or to the north. Freedom will be found in crossing the frontiers within and in changing the shape of the place in which we now live.

This is an advent time.

### New Year's Day, 1977

Quite an argument last night. We women closed ranks and said what we thought about the male clerical domination in the church. The men, the priests (Jim, Mark, and

Luigi), were quite hurt. Bill looked as if he didn't know whether he was innocent as a lay person or guilty for being male. Bill's girlfriend Susan called me "Attila the nun".

Thinking about it now, I'm sorry. We dumped all over them because they're the only ones who will listen without wiping us out in return. But they're not the problem; maybe even part of the solution. They don't like being part of the clerical class any more than we like being dominated by it.

My first few months working as a part-time chaplain at the university have drawn me once again into the nitty-gritty of church issues. However, I like being back in the thick of things at the Newman Centre — counselling, spiritual direction, and helping to organize a food co-op for the students and faculty who come to the centre. Have started preaching every other Sunday. The priest said he just couldn't carry the load alone. And it is a load. I'm still nervous about it — spend days preparing, write it all down, memorize, am exhausted Sunday night. And still usually feel I don't know what I'm talking about. There is a mystery here: when you try to speak about the gospel, there's a way in which you begin to hear it yourself. Anyway, the priest says it's a load off his mind and the people have been appreciative.

The experience has made me wonder if I would ever want to be ordained — presuming that day will come in the Roman Catholic church. I think not. I think my vocation is exactly what it is — to live as a member of a community, to try to respond to needs that aren't being met. Somehow, this is how I feel more free.

Most difficult aspect of the chaplaincy work: listening to the women who want to have an abortion. They're young, terrified, frantic, angry, and alone. What to say? How to be with them?

I told the others about my first contact with the gay

community. We all seem to be meeting more gay people now.

Two of the men at the Newman Centre asked me to speak to their "Dignity" group. Tried to explain that I didn't have much to say. They said they didn't want me to speak about homosexuality, just to give some reflections on the scriptures. "We can't get anyone to come. People are worried that they'll be labelled if they come to speak to us." I realized they were being treated like lepers, knew what Jesus would do. Went to the meeting and was disoriented for a while by whom I met and what I saw. Then they were just people.

*January 1977*
Now I know what discrimination means. It was a blow to all of us at the Newman Centre to get Archbishop Pocock's letter saying women could no longer preach in the archdiocese.

We've had many meetings. Will we resist? Will we comply? I'm ready to continue preaching. The problem is that the archbishop has said he'll remove the priestly faculties of the other chaplain if this happens. It would be cheap for me to take action if another has to pay the price. They control the system by controlling ordination, and then control all of us through the ordained. Why would any woman want to be ordained into this? I am becoming, as they say, an angry woman.

Many of the women who attend the liturgy at Newman feel as if they personally have been silenced—a visible sign that they have no voice in the church. Many are just walking away, voting with their feet. I felt powerless to do anything for them or for me. How little I have experienced such raw discrimination in my life. Nothing in my growing up prepared me for this. I never learned that being a woman made a difference—for better or worse. If there were difficulties, it was only a question of working harder or doing something to change the situation.

I know this silencing is wrong—not just for me but for all women in the church. I know it will change, because it's so obviously based on a lie. When? I don't know, but it will change. We are equal, created so by God. We are as much the church as the bishops. If anyone is going to leave the church it should be them, not us.

Given the pressure on the other chaplain, I know the best thing would be to resign at the end of the year. Besides, *Catholic New Times* is consuming more and more of my time. It seems we really do have a constituency out there, and somebody has to take the paper on in a more consistent way. I'll keep on preaching, just from a different pulpit.

## WOMEN: PRIESTS OR PROPHETS?
### (Editorial, CNT, Feb. 13, 1977)

The recent Vatican declaration has not put an end to the discussion regarding the ordination of women. If anything, it has brought the issue into sharper focus.

Women may be barred from the ranks of priests but they have been invited to join the company of prophets.

Throughout the scriptures, the prophets spoke God's word to kings and to priests. The words they spoke were both judging and promising. The prophets called on kings to be less embroiled in the world and on priests to be more related to life.

Surely women have a message to bring to the kings of this world. However, women also have something to say to the church of the priests.

Many of the first changes after Vatican II took place in the area of liturgical reform. A new vision of the church as a community related to life had to be expressed symbolically. Altars were turned around and the mass was conducted in the language of the people. These symbolic changes may have affected us in ways far deeper than we know.

In recent years a great deal of discussion has centred around who administers the sacraments. We have talked about ministers of communion, about deacons, about married priests, and, finally, about women priests. In retrospect, there seems to have been an unquestioned assumption that one had to become some kind of cleric in order to really serve in the church. Perhaps there was also some political sense that only a cleric had any real say in the decision-making process in the church, and that the group at the top of the hierarchical pyramid had to be expanded. But in the end this leaves the pyramid intact, and the laity, at the bottom of that pyramid, are left behind in the process. The great surge of lay movements in the fifties has been absorbed by this subtle form of clericalism. It is a clericalism which is as much a burden for priests as for anyone else.

It would be nice if women had an option on the present style of priesthood—an option to say NO. We would hope they would say no to this clerical domination—a structural dominance which is quite independent of the personal integrity of individual priests and bishops.

Women can say that NO only if it is encompassed by a larger YES. They must say yes to what is true in their own experience. Women need to affirm the ways in which they have carried crosses, healed the wounded, cared for the poor, and spoken God's message through the medium of their lives. It is in being faithful to these experiences that women will find the ways in which they can and do "resemble" Christ. The prophet knows that conditions must change in order for such a resemblance to be recognized.

The church must become a real community and not merely a symbolic one. The pyramid must become a circle. In a pyramid some are closer to Christ than others — clergy more than laity, men more than women, whites more than blacks, English more than French.... In a circle, each person is equidistant from the centre. In a community we all resemble Christ differently — but equally so. We have yet to discover what priesthood might mean in a communal church.

This is a New Time. It is a time for young women to prophesy and old women to dream dreams about a different kind of church and a different kind of world. It is a time for bold and fruitful action.

*February 1977*

One of the priests in the CNT working group came and told me that the archbishop was upset with our cartoon about women's ordination. The cartoon seemed innocent enough: Pope with pointy shoes sits on throne and listens as man carrying a cross is announced. "There's someone here who wants to speak to you about the priesthood of his mother." The priest said the archbishop told him to tell us that the paper would be closed if there was anything more like this.

Was it the pointy shoes!? First test: to back off on this is to begin the long retreat. Wrote the archbishop and told him I wanted to speak to him immediately about what the priest had communicated. Quoted back the archbishop's own words on paper. Never got a response.

Lesson: things mushroom in the dark. The hierarchy is used to dealing indirectly, and prefers to do so. Don't try to let your eyes adjust to the dark; get things out in the light where you can see what's going on.

*March 1977*
Notes from my plant book for an image of the church:
"Terrariums are completely self-enclosed containers in which plants and other living things can be maintained indefinitely. Because the containers prevent any outside disturbance, the plants are comfortably maintained with a perfect balance of water, soil, and gases from within this system. In this environment the plant's growth is stabilized so that one should not worry about the need to change the container."

*April 1977*
Propped up with pillows and pain-killers. My back gave out — too many twenty-hour days around production time. We can't go on like this. Can't keep up with the subscriptions coming in, the billing process. Can't keep generating stories, used up most of our contacts. Can't write fast enough — too anxious about committing myself in print. If I don't get better, if one more person gets sick, we won't have a production team.

Breathe. Remember the day when there was only $25 left in the account. You walked around the block and talked to God: "Listen, this is Your paper, it's up to You now." Remember the check for $20,000 that arrived the next day. Breathe, breathe easy.

*June 1977*
Ann and I went to a feminist retreat with a group of Protestant women. They thought it was so wonderful — to be just with women, to eat with women, to pray with women. Many said it was their dream come true.

Ann and I walked outside and laughed ourselves silly. We've both lived in women's communities for years and we didn't know we had it so good!

Maybe it's because of this experience that I am uncomfortable with the way these feminists idealize women. They seem to think women are more moral, more sensitive, more caring. It's just a newer variation of putting women up on some kind of pedestal. Surely we don't have to be "gooder" than men in order to justify our rights.

*July 1977*
Was it the sun that got under my skin? Was it the water, which pulled me out to where it met the sky? Was it the shell that broke in my hands? That day up north I knew I was grateful to be alive. I was amazed at each breath I took. Everything around me breathed a blessing, and I felt as if I too were a blessing. The trees waved to the heavens and the sun beamed back as I dove into the water, water all around, under and over. As I came to the surface, I thought that if this had been the only day of my life it would have been a very good life. "As in the beginning" I looked on this world "and saw that it was very good."

BEYOND ENTITLEMENT
(Editorial, CNT, Oct. 9, 1977)

Thanksgiving is more than just a time for turkey. Most Christians would nod their heads to that statement. Thanksgiving, we believe, is a time when we say "thank you" to God for all that we have received. However, it would seem that our "thank you" is more according to Emily Post than according to the gospel of Jesus. If we did render thanks in a deeply Christian way, the world would be a very different place. Saying "thank you" is not a social nicety. It can also be a difficult and dangerous thing to do. Why?

Robert Coles, a noted child psychologist, has been studying children from every social class in America for the last twenty years. He has been interested in the effects of social wealth and poverty on the psychological and moral development of children. His most recent book, *The Children of Affluence*, is instructive because most of us are children of affluence to some extent—even if only by adoption or by association in this culture.

Coles points out that "Wealth does not corrupt nor does it ennoble. But wealth does govern the minds of privileged children, giving them a peculiar kind of identity which they never lose, whether they grow up to be stockbrokers or communards, and whether they lead healthy or unstable lives" (*Atlantic Monthly*, Sept. 1977). He refers to the peculiar psychological trait associated with affluence as "entitlement". A child who has much wants and expects more—assuming it is his (hers) by right. This assumption gives the children of affluence a "belief" in their rights in whatever social sphere they choose to operate in. They feel entitled to wealth, power, education, leisure, beauty, solitude, etc. A child of affluence may devote himself or herself to charitable causes and still retain an attitude of entitlement. The rich young man may give up his possessions and go away sadly, wondering why he cannot follow Jesus. The rich young culture may give its money to the third world and wonder why nothing really seems to change.

This attitude of entitlement, formed by the social condition of affluence, is radically at odds with the attitude of thanksgiving that marks a Christian life as authentic.

Thanksgiving is the basic attitude of those who know themselves as creatures, who realize they are entitled to nothing. It is the attitude of those who believe that everything they have and are is a gift of the Creator. To be graceful is to live in the mystery of grace, letting it touch all the dimensions of our lives. Once we say "thank you" in this basically human way, we run a great risk.

Saying "thank you" implies that we have been given what we were not entitled to. Once we acknowledge our gifts, we are admitting that they can, and in some way must, be given away or shared. This is true of our material possessions, the advantages of position, the influence of education, the fulfilment of leisure, solitude, beauty, etc. Until a sense of gratitude filters through all the aspects of our lives, our prayers remain polite and our liturgies of thanksgiving are merely pretty. It seems that we who can afford so much can least afford to say "thank you".

Gratitude is the basis of a spiritual life, a truly human life which at the same time undercuts the basis of a materialistic culture. A spirituality which does not convert our social attitude of entitlement is polite, cultural Christianity. A political program which merely shifts the social basis of entitlement from one group to another cannot effect any enduring change. In all the dimensions of our lives we need to realize the paradox—that because no one is entitled, everyone is entitled.

Thank God.

*November 1977*
What is there to say except that I am deeply, passionately in love—probably have been so for some time. It was true from the first day, we just didn't want it to be true. It was true from the moment on that rainy day at the corner of St. George and Bloor when he offered to share his umbrella. And now we are both shaken, trembling. Wondering what this means, not wanting to wonder. Wanting to be married, wanting to keep the commitments we have already made. I suppose I should feel guilty but I don't. I'm grateful. If my life is to be shaken, better it be shaken by love.

There is no going back now. I can't just brush this off,

brush it aside. Now I know I can't direct my life by anything less than love.

*New Year's Day, 1978*
It seemed nearly everyone had something to say about celibacy last night. Jim told us he had fallen in love with a woman — will take a leave of absence from his dissertation and the priesthood to try to work it out. He wept as he told us. Being a priest isn't a role he plays from time to time — it's who he is. I never thought Jim would leave. It's very hard on Mark, his best friend. He seems to sense that this is what Jim must do but, like the rest of us, he feels sad and vulnerable. This has been the year when I learned men can cry.

After Jim, Isabel told us she had definitely decided to leave her community. We knew this was coming, although Isabel still can't seem to explain why she's making this move. But she seems more relaxed and happy. She has none of the anguish Jim has.

And we all know Ann is struggling to make her decision about final vows. She wondered out loud if she wasn't the fool. Dead silence.

Then Bill twanged his guitar and announced that he and Susan had got engaged at Christmas.

So we decided to celebrate it all — laughing, laughing through our tears.

Ann was right — taking a vow of celibacy is a very foolish thing to do these days. It doesn't make sense. Not sensible. That's the point, though. It has something to do with God, with whether God is real, whether God is love.

But I couldn't say that last night. I felt too tender. It bothered me, though; these are my friends. Something in me wants to be transparent, not just with them but with my community and others as well. My life is clouded with inconsistencies at the moment. Becoming transparent will mean making some choices.

What can I say now? Only this: that I believe God is Love and real enough to risk everything on that belief. And I am in love with this man, probably always will be. And I feel as if I will die if we are apart.

THE RESURRECTION FROM THE GARBAGE HEAP
(CNT, March 26, 1978)

I had never really thought about garbage before I went to Cairo. Now I wonder how I can think about the resurrection without remembering the garbage collectors of Cairo.

It was late at night when I flew into Cairo on a visit to a community of the Sisters of Our Lady of Sion. As I unpacked my bags in their small apartment, I pulled out my wad of travel brochures on the pyramids. I thought I knew what was worthwhile seeing in Egypt.

The next morning I woke up to the sound of honking cars and braying donkeys in the narrow street below. The smell of freshly baked bread drifted into the room. Over breakfast, one of the sisters invited me to visit—not the pyramids—but "the stable". The invitation sounded like a privileged one. "Most people in Cairo have never been to the stable." I accepted.

The train ride to the suburb of Matariya made riding the subways of Toronto seem like an exercise in gentility. People rode on the roof of the train, they hung on to the sides and exited through the windows. That's how it goes in a crowded city of eleven million people. However, with the exception of a few wealthy areas such as Heliopolis, Cairo is not a city in our sense of the word. It is more like a little village that has overgrown itself many times over. Public facilities such as bus, telephone, and traffic lights are problematic at best. It is not unusual to see poorly built apartment blocks collapse from the sheer wear and tear of living.

In the train station where we disembarked, I was obviously the tourist — with my blue eyes and a camera about my neck. However, no one came up to ask for money. Instead many people gestured to have their pictures taken. It struck me that I would have no way of sending the prints back to them, but that seemed beside the question. It was as if the most important thing was that someone would focus on their lives seriously for a moment — that someone would pick out their faces from the crowd and find them worthy of attention.

From the train station we walked along a winding dusty road for about a mile. Looking at the shacks on either side of the road, I kept thinking, "Surely we must be there...it can't get any worse." But we continued on.

Eventually we came to a clearing and all I could see was a brown mound in the distance. "That is the stable," my companion told me. As we came closer to the mound, I realized — by the smell and by the flies — that this garbage heap was "the stable". The brown mound appeared to cover at least two square miles. We went up on the mound and through it along a series of twisting paths that led us into the world of the garbage collectors.

It became apparent that this decaying mass of garbage was alive — with flies, with rats, with pigs, with donkeys — and with people. The heap was inhabited. The places called home squatted on top of the garbage. Jigsaws of cardboard and metal sheets held up roofs which were a latticework of rags.

At first I could see nothing but the poverty. Everything — the people, the animals, and the houses — seemed to be sinking into the garbage. I felt a sinking feeling within myself. A cry burst inside me — "Jesus!" It was more of an accusation than a pious prayer.

Ahead of me on the path were two small children going through the garbage on the ground. A little girl was eating a rotten tomato. Rats the size of cats were nosing through the garbage next to a little boy.

It would have been easy to get fixated on the rats but I became more fascinated by the children. Their beautiful faces radiated a kind of transparent peace. They looked up and greeted me with a smile — "*Zayda.*" I felt less of a foreigner.

Talking to my companion along the way, I learned more about the inhabitants of the garbage heap. There were about 15,000 garbage collectors living there. Most of them had come from Upper Egypt, where their thin slices of land had not been sufficient to live on. Illiterate, without papers, they sought refuge in this left-over place. Many of them have lived here for generations. Early every morning, they leave for Cairo on their carts drawn by pathetic little donkeys. Each cart has a certain "beat", a certain territory of the city to be covered. And of course some areas are more profitable than others.

Usually the garbage collectors work in teams — a man and a child. One sits and watches the garbage while the other goes to the doors of the houses for the garbage. The carts can be seen everywhere in Cairo — often incongruously parked next to the limousine of a Saudi Arabian prince. The carts return to the garbage heap before the midday traffic begins in the city, and then each family sorts the garbage from its cart — food for the family, food for the animals, clothes, furnitures, pieces of metal, glass, and paper. Some of the garbage will be used by the family, some will be sold for a small sum, and some will be recycled. Occasionally a treasure is discovered but usually the garbage from this poor city makes for rather slim pickings.

Garbage sorting becomes the occasion for small acts of hostility and generosity.

This daily routine never varies. If a garbage collector misses a day, the family and animals will go hungry. As a result, many of them have never seen the Nile—or the pyramids. Nevertheless, by Cairo standards the garbage collectors do have a certain dignity—their work is necessary and it is consistent. Until a few years ago, there would have been little more to say about the garbage collectors. The mysteries of their loves and sufferings were tied to the cycle of the garbage.

Finally we came to a stop in front of two little square rooms which had a kind of clearing around them. A swing dangled from some poles in the clearing. "This is the school and this is where Sister Emmanuelle lives."

I stepped inside the doorway of the school. Although there was only a two-foot-square window, the whole room seemed lit up with the smiles of the fifty children. There was no danger of anyone falling off a seat because they were all squeezed in so tightly along two long benches. Like children everywhere, they were learning the alphabet—"*Aleph, be, the, se.*" Three young Arab teachers eagerly showed me the drawings and the sewing done by the children. I had a real sense that the teachers and the pupils were tremendously proud of what they were doing. When the children learned the alphabet they would be able to go to the government-supported schools, and after that—who knows what else?

On the door of the school was a cross and the words in Arabic "*Allah mahabba*"—God is Love.

The school is one of the many works of love of Sr. Emmanuelle. She was not there when I visited the garbage heap, but from my conversations with the people I sensed that she was, as they said, "our sister".

Sr. Emmanuelle's is a riches-to-rags story. A graduate

of the Sorbonne in Classics and a Sister of Sion, she taught for years in the Middle East, in schools for Arab girls from wealthy families. When she was in Alexandria, the contrast between the elegant and quiet school and the poor neighbourhood surroundings became intolerable to her. She asked to live with a poor family and soon started a school for the poor in the neighbourhood. Eventually the school came of age and she turned it over to a community of Coptic Christian sisters.

At sixty-one years of age, Sr. Emmanuelle hoped to give the last years of her life to the lepers. However, the lepers were living in what had become a military zone after the 1967 war. A curious series of circumstances led her instead to the garbage collectors of Cairo. She has lived with them for nine years — and loved them. According to her, these have been the happiest years of her life. "The poor have evangelized me," she says.

Sr. Emmanuelle eats with the garbage collectors, works with them, laughs with them, prays with them. Indeed, she considers herself to be a garbage collector: the title of the book describing her life with them translates as *Rag Picker with the Rag Pickers*.

Reading her lively book, one is struck by her unique appreciation of each of the garbage collectors. There is Fauzeya, the mother of many who recites the gospel before going to bed. There is Guirguis, who is depressed by his work. There is Fawzi, who bought a candy for his mother instead of for himself. There is Mohmound, who forgave those who killed his brother.

Between Moslems and Christians living in "the stable" Sr. Emmanuelle has brought a sense of understanding and trust. To the women she has given a sense of dignity. She has attracted medical students to start a clinic and teachers to expand the school to include courses for the adults. She has encouraged the garbage collectors to work in a more collective way so that they can free each other to go to school in the evenings or to go to the pyramids for a holiday. At the present moment, Sr. Emmanuelle is in Switzerland investigating the possibility of turning the residue of the garbage into fertilizer.

Writing from Switzerland to some of her friends about the project, Sr. Emmanuelle concluded: "Yes, the world is beautiful. Its song of love resounds. It is not the clang of violence or hatred but the little reed flute that makes the forest ring. It mingles with the songs of Christ as Victor over death. God in heaven hears it and redeems all people."

As I came down from the mound, the garbage collectors were sorting through the goods they had gathered that day. I knew they had taught me something that had never been given through prayer or my own experience. I understood something about sin, about redemption, and about resurrection that I had never heard in theology courses.

About sin: the fact is that so much high-priced garbage in the world keeps some human beings in the position of being forever garbage collectors. The day I went to the garbage heap was the same day the United States promised to sell F-15 bombers to Egypt. The war with Israel is a rather meaningless exercise for the garbage collectors of Cairo. War is what is talked about in strategy sessions and cocktail parties, what happens in the sky and on the desert. Far more important is the price of bread, which jumps every time a new bomber is purchased.

About redemption: nothing is ever completely useless. Nothing and no one is a leftover to be thrown away. It can all be reclaimed as a source of life and energy.

About resurrection: it is simply a fact that in the midst of a garbage heap in Cairo there is a school which says "God is Love" on the door.

I never saw the pyramids. I didn't need to.

*April 1978*
Devastating letter from the School of Graduate Studies. I've been kicked out of the program because of "lack of evidence" of any "progress" on the dissertation. Yes, the evidence is lacking. The only evidence I have is that we have started a little newspaper and it has progressed. Not evidence of "serious" work! Wobbled over to Gregory Baum's office. He got me some coffee and helped me get my act together. After a few phone calls it was clear: either I take some time off and finish the thesis or that's it. I dread but want to do it and think I'm ready for it. The work at *Catholic New Times* has given me a sharper sense of the need to reflect on the events in these times. I can't just go from issue to issue without taking time to consider the deeper questions involved. Now I have something to think about, some questions that need answers. The challenge will be to find a way of focusing in on these.

*May 1978*
You think you're working for the poor and then you realize you don't know the first thing about it. I was grousing around the office complaining to Mary Power about the lack of equipment — one phone, one desk, one typewriter — and about how tacky the paper looked because of what we had to work with. "Well," she smiled wisely, "only the rich can afford to be efficient."

That means: if you're going to work for the poor you may have to work as the poor. There's something I've come to terms with, something I've made peace with.

*May 1978*
Went to a conference for Catholics United for the Faith in London, Ontario. Wanted to see the whites of their conservative eyes. Scary. They're convinced they're right.

A lot of people seem comforted by such certitude. Perhaps we need to take more notice. Interviewed Bishop Emmett Carter, who has just been made Archbishop of Toronto. He said it was unfortunate that in recent years bishops have failed to speak with authority. "However," Carter added, "some of us have recovered our voice." We are in for some interesting times.

A curious incident at the conference: an older lady came up to me and asked if I had joined CUFF yet. To which I replied, "Well, I'm really only here as a journalist." "Oh," said the lady, somewhat confused, "I thought you were one of us." Then she smiled broadly. "Well, of course you are. You're one of God's children." She was sincere.

TALKING ABOUT DEATH
(CNT, June 4, 1978)

Dr. Elisabeth Kübler-Ross broke a sound barrier several years ago when she began to talk openly about death. On Saturday May 27, echoes of that breakthrough reverberated throughout Convocation Hall at the University of Toronto. She spoke generally about the experience of death and the evidence for life after death. Drawing on her vast clinical experience, Kübler-Ross focused particularly on children, and on how they relate to death.

Throughout her talk, an older man in the audience, with a childlike expression, seemed to second everything she was saying. He was John Howard Griffin, the well-known civil rights leader and author of *Black Like Me*. Griffin, who had introduced Kübler-Ross, was less vocal but equally persuasive in conveying a powerful message to the people who had come.

In his opening remarks, Griffin recalled that he had

read Kübler-Ross's writings at an earlier time, when he was more concerned with the living. At that time, he had read her work from "the other side of the fence". Now Griffin, who is seriously ill, reads "from this side of the fence". He described his fatigue with the facile remarks that many make about suffering and death, and his joy in finding someone who could speak in a language he could understand. This slight, fifty-year-old woman was a significant person for Griffin because "the most neglected minority of all are the people who are terminally ill."

Throughout her lecture, Kübler-Ross, who refers to herself as a "Swiss hillbilly", called on people to face the pain involved in living — and in dying. "If you shield the canyon from the windstorms, you will never see the beauty of its caverns."

Repeating the approach she has set forth in her book *On Death and Dying*, Kübler-Ross emphasized the importance of not sedating ourselves against the guilt and anger of death. Developing this further, she pointed out that adults must be careful not to pass on their accumulated fears about death to children.

Kübler-Ross gave an example of how she would explain death, and life after death, to a child: "Your mommy is in a cocoon. When the time is right, the cocoon opens up and out of it comes a butterfly."

In summarizing the results of her research, Kübler-Ross said that those who have been pronounced clinically dead and have recovered have reported a sense of shedding their physical body and of finding a new and perfect body. "The blind see, the lame walk, and the retarded have a new sense of wisdom." These people have a feeling of peace and serenity and a sense of being in the presence of an unconditional love. In this love one never "dies" alone, but rather one feels united with those one loves. In this love, one reviews the whole of one's life and the true meaning of it becomes clear. If there is any condemnation, says Kübler-Ross, it is only because "you condemn yourself."

*June 1978*
It has become clear, painfully clear. We cannot get married. All the things that drew us to each other are now drawing us apart — our faith, our hopes. We must put some long distance between ourselves. We are still struggling to understand and yet we do understand. It has everything to do with love, everything to do with God. There is something I have learned which it seems I needed to learn and learned only with this person: love, vulnerability, suffering. We have both learned to cry.

Now I will never be tempted to be a professional church person. I will never be content with just doing good work. I will never be satisfied with being a left-wing politico. I owe it to him, I owe it to us, to let my life be directed by love. If I don't, then this decision will leave my soul in dust and ashes.

I am left with this emptiness that perhaps not even God can fill. Will God bring an umbrella for the rain?

Yet somehow I trust that God is not playing tricks on us. I trust that we will be sustained by a loving presence even while we are absent from one another. Maybe someday we may even be friends. For now that seems impossible. And so I have put him on a plane for a refugee camp on the Cambodian border. And I am left waving, wavering, waving.

*July 1978*
Rome. Have been here a month. I thought I would never survive having to stay here for so long on community business. The whole institutional church scene is absolutely suffocating. Everyone hangs on every word the Pope

says. They don't know that few are listening elsewhere. There is lots of pomp and pageantry for the pious who flock to the city. Theatre. The city is rife with gossip and rumours, wheeling and dealing, and all in the name of God. It's as Hegel said: "When politics is dismissed from the front door of the church it returns again through the sanctuary."

Still, I have discovered another Rome – the flowers, the golden glow over the city in the late afternoon, the laughter in the streets, the pizza, the English-language flicks at the Pasquino, where the roof rolls open to let in some air – and then the poor and some of the most vital Christian communities I have ever seen. Rome, like the church, is all of this.

## THE CHURCH OF THE CATACOMBS
### (CNT, Sept. 10, 1978)

In the city of Rome today there is a centre and there is a periphery. The tourist, pilgrim, and cameraman usually see only the centre of Rome – the splendid Vatican, the rich museums, the chic shopping areas, the historic churches, and the beautiful residences which have been restructured within ancient walls.

The poor live on the periphery of this city's centre. And, as in the time of the first apostles, there are still Christians in the "catacombs" on the outskirts of Rome. In tiny communities they worship in the hollowed-out basements of flimsy apartment blocks. In small working groups, they preach the gospel to people who have become unbelievers in this most Catholic of cities.

As the sun sets, it creates its famous golden glow over the centre of Rome. At the same time, the sun casts its shadows over the dreary concrete blocks which are home for over 1.5 million poor on the periphery. Every Roman loves the sun, and flowers, and music—but not everyone can enjoy them.

Rome is eternal—so they say. There are always the rich, the powerful, the artists, the priests of the official religion—and the poor. This is the enduring truth of Rome. In the midst of this reality there is also a persistent hope which is continually being reborn from the dust of its suffering and struggles.

Today, this city which is the official centre of Catholicism is also the centre of a seething social despair. Inflation continues and unemployment on the periphery is over 40 per cent. For most of those who are out of work, unemployment insurance is not a possibility. Any young person who finishes school is forced to say, "There is no place for me. There is no work." The Christian Democratic Party, which has ruled Italy for over thirty years, is generally considered corrupt in some of its practices, and the Catholic church as an institution has become increasingly "peripheral" to the lives of the people.

Given this social situation, the Communist Party is rapidly gaining ground, and the terrorists of the Red Brigade have mounted their program of kidnapping, assassination, and kneecap shootings.

One wonders if anything good can come out of Rome....

And yet in Rome today there is an incredible hope against hope which is manifesting itself in grassroots groups throughout the city. One such group is the community of St. Egidio, which has been described by the French theologian Yves Congar as "the future of the church" and by others as "a new form of monasticism". It began with ten high-school students in 1968, the year of the violent student revolts throughout Europe. Gianni La Bella, one of the original group of ten, describes the electric atmosphere of that time in this way: "It was a world marked deeply by an anxiety for something new, and by a strong criticism of everything which had been built by others. It was a world in which there was a deep distance from the church and a mistrust for everything connected with it."

These ten blue-jeaned students, boys and girls from a middle-class school in Rome, turned to the scriptures at one point in their critical search. Most of them had never really read that book. They asked, "Does this have anything to say to us?" The scriptures seemed to suggest an answer or, at least, a way of response. In a rather disorganized fashion, the students continued to discuss the scriptures, and soon others joined them. When they continued on to university, the students formed a group which met in the morning to pray with the gospels and the psalms. Eventually, the motley group began to see itself as a *familia Dei*, a family of God. While other radical students mocked this little "family", its members were beginning to ask themselves a concrete question — "Is this gospel possible to live here in Rome?"

This question led the students to the periphery of the city. It was a shocking encounter in some ways. They met people who were as alienated as themselves from the institutions of church and society. It was in this encounter that the students' group moved beyond the temporary communal experiences and the short-lived radical efforts of the sixties.

From the very beginning, the students knew that they could not just go and work for the poor on the periphery. They sensed that they had to commit themselves to forming community, in a concrete way, with these people.

The people on the periphery had been repeatedly disappointed by political activists who had come to try out some new theory which they had learned in the classroom — and then moved on to more exciting things. These activists were called *infami*, or traitors. Their abstract categories of "the people" or "the proletariat" seemed to make them uncaring about the concrete sufferings of people, and blinded them to the well-springs of hope that existed within the people on the periphery.

The young men and women from the student quarter and the people from the periphery met each other in a faltering way at first. After a time of testing they became fellow-workers, and then — friends. They found that they enjoyed being together and that each person had unique gifts to bring to the task at hand in the "third world of Rome".

In 1973, the loosely knit student community had become so large that it was increasingly difficult to find a place in which to meet. While some of the students had gone to live on the periphery, others continued to live at home or in small communities in the apartments of the student quarter. Just when the students were beginning to feel the necessity for a central place in which to pray and to plan, an old monastery became vacant in the Trastevere district; the monks had simply died off. The students moved in — with the blessing of the bishop.

The old monastery was on a narrow side street surrounded by bars and pizzerias. It was only a stone's throw from the Vatican "palace" for Justice and Peace and from Santa Maria in Trastevere, the oldest Christian church in Rome. The monastery was called St. Egidio (St. Giles). And so the nameless student group and the sprouting families of God came to be called the "Community of St. Egidio". No one really lived in the monastery. It was used as a place of prayer, a storage house for a food co-op, a school for delinquents, a centre for study — and the site of the best party in the Trastevere on Saturday night, when motor-scooters and mopeds lined its front entrance.

The community chose St. Egidio as a centre — but not in order to stay in the centre of the city. The monastery became the centre because it gave the students easy access to all the quarters on the periphery. In turn, it became the meeting place for the communities which had developed on the periphery.

The community of St. Egidio did not begin with an idea, nor did it proceed according to some master plan. Like Topsy, it just grew. Nevertheless, this growth was not without a certain amount of reflection. Conscious choices were made regarding the life and work of the community. The community reached into the rich storehouse of tradition in the church, and brought this to bear on their concrete experience in the city.

The community referred back to the rule of Saint Benedict for inspiration for their life together.

Some of the musicians at St. Egidio began to compose songs that expressed their faith in the midst of the city. These songs are not "folk songs" nor do they have any musical accompaniment. They are haunting and buoyant compositions which seem to resonate with the Gregorian chant sung by the monks of former days. However, there the comparison ends — the monks never sang so loudly, nor with such gusto!

Artists at St. Egidio turned to the icons of the Eastern Church as a way of assisting the prayer of their community — a community which included many illiterate people, who were more responsive to an image than to the written word.

There are surprisingly few problems in the St. Egidio community. Enthusiasm and good humour pervade most of its activities. It is a time of great generosity, high risk, and enormous creativity. Clearly the members of St. Egidio are delighted with what they are doing together, and most of them are in it for the long haul. "Our problem is the city of Rome," they say.

The high-spiritedness of the St. Egidio community is not because of the temper of the times. One no longer sees the optimistic slogans that were painted on the walls of Rome in '68— "Imagination Is Power". Now one sees messages like "My name is Paul. I am all alone and I have no future."

In dealing with the problems of the periphery in 1978, the community of St. Egidio has to be both patient and perceptive. Most of the inhabitants are immigrants from southern Italy who come to the city seeking work. For those who do find work, the pay is low, and the four hours spent commuting each day create an endless cycle of fatigue.

Many of the men have had to move again, to Germany or to Arab countries, to find work—leaving behind many women and children. Most of the immigrants are illiterate, speaking in a dialect from the south. Thirty-eight per cent of the families on the periphery have more than six children, most of whom will drop out of school because they cannot handle the Italian language and they are unable to relate to the curriculum, which is geared to children living in the centre of Rome. Because of the high rate of illiteracy, many people do not even have the dignity of having their births and deaths recorded. There are not enough schools to educate the children of the periphery; in the quarter of Nuova Ostia, for example, there is one elementary school for 50,000 people.

Education was a key to change on the periphery. At first the students worked with dropouts in the evening. Then they realized that these students would continue to drop out unless something was done about the curriculum in the schools. A group from St. Egidio developed a whole curriculum for "popular schools".

And where did all this take place? There was no room in the quarters for classrooms or a school—so they went underground! The community in each quarter hollowed out the dirt basement of a large apartment block. They had only simple tools, and sometimes they used their bare hands. Walls were constructed, and soon there was a whole underground complex of classrooms, meeting rooms, and a chapel. In the tradition of the early Christians, they met underground, on the outskirts of the city, in a place which had become a burial ground.

The members of the community of St. Egidio have chosen the more difficult path and have stayed in the city of Rome—because it is there that they find people and it is there that they find God. Gianni La Bella explains this further by referring to the fact that Saint Benedict did not go out to the desert to escape people—he went out to meet the devil. "Today the city has become a desert similar to the one in the scriptures. It is much easier to see desolation and solitude in the human desert of the city than in the natural one. For us, the lonely place where one looks for God is inside the city. We must find new ways of expressing our faith, of praying, of being together, in spite of the haste, the noise, the lack of space. A minority church lives in the city the experience of the desert— it is here that hunger, nostalgia, and idolatry tempt her."

*September 1978*
Looking back over this time at the newspaper, I want to say YES to it all. Yes to the frustration, yes to the late hours, yes to the insecurity. It's all part of the birth process we've engaged in together. What has been born

is so tiny and fragile — very much like the church we hope in.

Something has come to birth in me as well. I've been forced out of some self-protective space. I've been pushed to say who I am and what I stand for. And that has been exhilarating. There is lots I'm still unsure about and maybe the time working on the dissertation will help me sort some of that out.

And what has been true on one level has been even more true on another. I have been forced to say who I am to God and to the man I love. I may not be sure who I am but I do know why.

# II

## The Dead of Night

*Thanksgiving Day, 1978*
There is no end in sight. I have been reading for months
now, turning back page after page of the history of the
Holocaust. I can't read the lines and I can't read between
the lines. A kind of numbness has settled in somewhere
between my eyes. The facts have become familiar, too
familiar. It's only the faces that thaw my mind — a picture
here, a story there. It's the faces of children that search
me out and ask, "What would you have done?"

I have no answer. I sit in my room like some distant
spectator, watching as so many watched, watching as the
churches and governments watched, watching as God
watched.

I try to write and my typewriter sounds like a machine
gun in the silence.

This was supposed to be a thesis but now I think it will
finish me before I ever finish it. Now I have really been
silenced — not by the church but by reality.

Yet something in me refuses to close the book on all of

this. As far as the dissertation is concerned, I am drawn along by the only significant question I heard posed in all the philosophy courses at graduate school. It was Emil Fackenheim's question: "How can we keep on doing philosophy in the same way after the event of the Holocaust?" And I am also asking, "How can I keep on believing in the same way after what I know happened?" I thought I knew something about the darker side of the church but I think I saw it more as weakness. The church has always been such an encircling source of life and hope for me that I have been unshaken by its more obvious weaknesses.

But I cannot deny that the church which preaches universal love has also nourished a particular hatred for the Jewish people. From what I have read, it seems clear that in the Nazi era the church acted more out of a desire to protect its institutional self-interest than out of a commitment to helping those marked for death.

I can't write but I can't stop thinking about what happened to those six million people. In fact, I am probably thinking more deeply than I have in years. I am thinking about why I can't think, thinking that this reality has shattered all our previous categories of philosophical thought.

Hannah Arendt has given me the courage to keep on thinking even as I draw yet another blank. I've decided to focus on her writings about the Holocaust because she had the courage to let her philosophy be shaken and shaped by this event. Courage — something born in the heart that can grow up in the mind.

There's not much I can feel thankful for this Thanksgiving, except the little thesis support group that Ann, Isabel, and I have formed. We've made a commitment to see each other through this process. There's hardly anyone else (other than my community) that I see these days. We meet once a week and share the work we have done.

I don't have much to share but the meetings help me sustain the tension of the question.

*New Year's Day, 1979*
Lots of speculation last night about the new pope, John Paul II. He's certainly interesting. Mark said the conservatives had finally got one of their own in place. Nobody else was that alarmed. Somehow I doubt the conservatives wield that much power any more.

In any case, I'm not a fan of the papacy these days. The more I read about what Pius XII did and did not do during the time of the Holocaust, the more I'm convinced that he was guided more by this fear of Communism than by any real horror of what the Nazis were doing. There seems to be something in the very structure of the church that makes it more comfortable with Fascism than with Communism.

The good news is that Jim was able to make it up from the States with his new wife. Great opportunity to celebrate his new job as a city planner. What a switch for him — from studying Saint Thomas Aquinas' notion of happiness to managing a small town in the Midwest. Jim says there are lots of philosophical and theological considerations in planning a town. The people there have probably never had anyone so concerned about the quality of life.

More good news: some of the group are really moving ahead on their dissertations. They're sounding more assured, beginning to think about what lies ahead.

I still haven't written a thing. But some convictions are slowly forming within me as I continue to read through Hannah Arendt:

• The twentieth century is a hoax. Who can believe in the

myth of progress or in the moral superiority of this age after the Holocaust?

- The Holocaust was not an aberration but a manifestation of the truth of the twentieth century — its socio-economic and political systems.
- It happened in a system in which human beings were separated from one another and from the consequences of their own actions. It was a system in which nice and ordinary people contributed to an evil of great consequence.
- It happened in a system of organized guilt — everyone was made complicit but few felt any sense of responsibility.
- It happened in a system which was structured so that the oppressors often felt themselves to be victims of it. The system was organized so that the victims were often made to participate in their own process of oppression.
- It happened because so many participated in the system. Simply by participating, you make it work. Unless you are working to correct the faults of a system, then you are helping it to function.
- It happened because so many good people abdicated responsibility for public life and retreated to their tiny private worlds of personal purpose.
- The Nazis had only as much authority as people gave them. Whenever people withdrew their consent, the authority weakened.
- It is too easy to cast Hitler as the evil demon who was responsible. More perplexing: the possibility that he was a rather ordinary person.
- Some people acted on behalf of the victims. We think of them as exceptional. But such a thought gives no consolation. They were indeed exceptions that proved the general rule — so many did nothing.
- The significance of ideology: ideology is always consis-

tent. Reality is never that consistent. Propaganda: anything repeated often enough becomes true.

- Human rights are meaningless abstractions unless they have legal and political guarantees. When the rights of one group are threatened, the rights of all are potentially in jeopardy.
- The darkness of the Holocaust is not just a void, not just the absence of light. It is a humanly constructed and manufactured darkness.

*January 1979*

Visited our community in Spain on my way to another meeting in Rome. The country is so intense: sharp colours, sharp feelings. It made me realize how moderate we are in our doubts, how we believe within reason. Insipid. Spain has more than its share of mystics and fanatics. Is it possible to have a culture with a passionate love for God without the passionate desire to hate?

Toledo was like a city arising from a dream. Here and there were signs of the Golden Age when Christians and Jews and Moslems lived together in peace and created something of great beauty. Yet the Inquisition also had its day here. The golden ages seem so brief in the dark length of history. But they have happened — every now and then.

*March 1979*

Received a call from Tom Harpur (the Religion editor of the *Toronto Star*) asking if I would be willing to contribute to a regular column.

I don't want to. Partly because I still feel I have so little to say, and partly because I need to keep focused on the thesis. I'm not ready. It's not the time.

You'll never be ready. If you're honest it's also self-protective. It's one thing to write for a little lefty ghetto

Catholic newspaper and another thing to write for the largest newspaper in the country.

I would be exposed, vulnerable, a persona that people would project their dreams and nightmares onto. Especially if it's about religion, especially as I'm a woman, especially as I'm a nun.

My sense is that 20 per cent of the readers will canonize me, 20 per cent will hate me, and the rest won't care.

Yet how can I say no after all these months in the dark? How can I not take some responsibility for public life?

The question brings to the surface the pleasant memory of all those long days of silence in the novitiate, when I did nothing more than pray and do housework. My religious commitment seems to be taking me in such a different direction from the way it started out. That was when silence seemed so full, when it was the beginning, not the ending, of words. That was when everything I did was directed towards one goal — the glory of God. And now I don't think of God as so glorious. I see God dragged through the course of time, splattered with the mud of human history. And I see no other option than to get a little muddied.

*June 1979*

Went to visit Mary McCarthy (Hannah Arendt's literary executor) in Paris while on my way to a meeting in Rome. It was interesting to hear about the group of people who circled around the *Partisan Review* in the early fifties in New York. Sounded a little bit like *Catholic New Times*.

It was also interesting to hear about Hannah from a friend. I told Mary that Emil Fackenheim didn't like Arendt very much because she had never criticized her teacher Heidegger for his pro-Nazi stance. I told her Fackenheim thinks that Arendt is "soft-headed". Mary said that wasn't the case; "Hannah wasn't soft-headed, she was soft-hearted. She had an affair with Heidegger and his Nazi wife forced him to break off the relationship with this young Jewish student." What you don't know from books!

Mary kept asking me why I wasn't wearing a habit. It was as if she wanted to get me back in the box with all her "memories of a Catholic girlhood"!

TORONTO THE HOLY?
(*Toronto Star* [TS], June 30, 1979)

The only time I ever heard of "Toronto the Holy" was eleven years ago, in a remote Indian village in the Northwest Territories.

It was the summer of 1968. Having just finished my undergraduate studies in western Canada, I volunteered to supervise a group of high-school students who would be running a recreation program for Indian children. We went north that summer with all our liberal illusions about "helping those less fortunate than ourselves". We learned that the people there lived by some illusions too — but these were more akin to prophetic dreams.

The settlement on the Mackenzie River was so remote that it had remained relatively untouched by the ways of the south. Life was more difficult for them because of that distance. In visiting the village burial grounds, we discovered that many children died from TB and pneumonia. Even some adults did not survive an unusually long and harsh winter. However, life was also more religious for them because of that isolation. For all their hardships, they were neither anxious nor bored.

They had a way of caring for each other which challenged the kind of "charity" we gave from the leftovers of our lives. I remember watching a group of young boys who had spent a whole day hauling in a huge Arctic grayling from the river. In the evening, when the fish finally flopped onto the shore, the boys cut it into equal pieces. Then the boys delivered one piece to each of the shacks in the village. No one owned the fish, and no one owned the river. Thus everyone had a right to share in the feast of the fish. They never dreamed that there was any other way of doing things.

The village was unusually Christian. An old Oblate priest had lived with those people for more than fifty years. He had learned their ways and they had listened to his words. The only real contact the old priest had with the church outside the village was through the Bible and the few books he had brought with him from the seminary in France. But in 1968 he received a copy of the documents of the Second Vatican Council — five years after the meeting had taken place.

One Sunday morning, we sat with the people in their little church and listened to his sermon on Vatican II. In halting phrases he said something like this:

"My dear brothers and sisters, I have just received news of a great meeting which has taken place in Rome. All our bishops met to talk about faith and about love. They have written many things about the Spirit and about Jesus. But I must confess that I don't understand these writings very well. There are many big words like 'secularization' and 'revelation'. I am not very learned and not very holy. But I want us to understand these writings because I believe they will help us to love one another more.

"I am not discouraged, though, because I believe there are many holy and learned men in places like Toronto, in the south, who do understand. They will show us how to live better and to love."

Two years later, I came to Toronto to see and hear for myself. I have met Toronto the good, the bad, and the ugly. I have heard many learned men. But I have never seen the holy city. I don't know if I see more, or if I see less, than those people did.

Perhaps they too see things differently now, for the ways of the south have moved north. The Mackenzie Valley Pipeline has been charted to pass right through that village.

A NEW SPIRIT OF TRIUMPHALISM?
(TS, July 28, 1979)

I was a little spooked by some recent remarks of Bishop Lewis S. Garnsworthy. He is quoted as saying that he senses a "new spirit of triumphalism" in the Roman Catholic Church. Strong words from the Anglican Bishop of Toronto. They raised the ghosts of the Catholic past — ghosts I thought were being laid to rest.

Bishop Garnsworthy seemed to suggest that the Roman Catholic Church was not reaching out, in humility, to join in an ecumenical dialogue with other Christian churches. Instead, Rome was "taking up the drawbridges" and waiting for other Christians to come to it — on Rome's terms. This "new spirit of triumphalism" was supported by the feeling among Catholics that they had a winner in the attractive person of Pope John Paul II.

Bishop Garnsworthy's statement would imply that the Roman Catholic Church had lowered its drawbridges when it was losing its battle with the wicked world. Only in the face of impending defeat did its beleaguered forces go out in search of Christian allies. This would reduce the ecumenical movement to a survival tactic on the part of the Roman Catholic Church.

A sad comment — but is it true?

If Bishop Garnsworthy is right that there is a new spirit

of triumphalism in the Roman Catholic Church, it is wrong to conclude that this means it is winning. This triumphalism indicates that the church may be losing in a far deeper sense. Drawbridges are raised, not in confidence, but in fear.

There is a lot of free-floating fear in the air these days: human relations have never seemed more fragile, and our economic situation is moving beyond our control. There is little confidence that tomorrow will be better than today.

In fear, people search for clarity to protect themselves from the confusion that swirls about them. They turn to cults, movements, political ideologies, and psychological analysis for "the answers". They may even turn to a church — not because it has the best answer, but because it has the clearest answer.

In such a situation, the church with the clearest answers may well seem triumphant. But the victory is illusory. A flock that is formed through fear will not find its deepest fears assuaged by clear answers.

If we are to believe the scriptures, only love casts out fear. Only Christian communities of love can respond to the deepest fears of our contemporary world. The answer of Christianity is love. That is not a clear answer, but it is a real one.

A fearful church will indeed "raise the drawbridges" and shun ecumenical dialogue. There are too many problems, too many unanswered questions, involved in such a discussion.

However, a loving church will lower the drawbridges and go out to embrace fellow Christians, the men and women of today. Love is expansive, not protective. Love believes in its own power. Triumphalism is not the sign of confidence — it is the mask of fear.

From where I sit, in my uncomfortable pew, I see that Pope John Paul II represents different things to different

Catholics: he is either the man with the expansive heart, or the man with all the answers.

I also see that Rome symbolizes different things to Catholics. At its best, it expresses our desire to let our hearts expand beyond the fortresses created by national and cultural boundaries. At its worst, it becomes the head office of the branch plant Canadian Catholic Church.

In my opinion, the ecumenical dialogue will go forward, primarily because of the saints — the gentle, fiery, faithful lovers — who enliven the different Christian traditions. This movement of love can be helped or hindered by theologians, committees, and bishops.

Is Bishop Garnsworthy right that there is a "new spirit of triumphalism" in the Roman Catholic Church? I suspect your answer will depend on the company you keep.

## PASSION PLAY IS THE PITS
### (TS, Nov. 17, 1979)

The Passion Play is the pits. That's putting it mildly — and a little less judiciously than Rabbi Jordan Pearlson did in this column a few weeks ago.

Rabbi Pearlson raised his voice against the continuing anti-Semitism in the world-famous Oberammergau play which will be re-enacted in Germany this summer. Amen, brother.

However, amens are easy to say. Actions are a little harder to come by. Indeed it would seem that many efforts on the part of Christians and Jews alike to change the basic prejudice of this play have failed.

It is true that the language of the play has been cleaned up a little but the basic structure of the play is indelibly marked by the image of the Jews as Christ-killers. This myth of the Christ-killers has provided the backdrop against which many Christians have become Jew-killers.

I cannot applaud the Oberammergau play as a drama of redemptive love, because it perpetuates a particular hatred. I have fantasies of throwing something rotten to the core. The continuing anti-Semitism of the play makes a mockery of the passion of Christ. The play provides a possible prelude to the real suffering of Jewish people. I am sure that Jesus, the Jew, would never have taken part in this play.

The Oberammergau play perpetuates the passion of the Jewish people. They have walked the way of the cross too often. Not long ago they walked to the Golgotha of the modern world — Auschwitz. Christians must stop giving Jews more crosses to bear.

Of course, as long as Christians continue to play with the myth of the Jews as Christ-killers, the personal and institutional sinfulness of Christianity can be avoided. Christians have crucified Christ many times over, in the Jews, in the the poor, in those who are different.

After Auschwitz, the Oberammergau play is not only obscene — it is a diabolical drama. After Auschwitz, no passion play should be produced which could not be staged with integrity in front of Jewish survivors of the murder camps. The Oberammergau play should close after the first night.

Yet the show will go on this summer. Travel agencies in Toronto have been advertising "pilgrimages" to Oberammergau. This dark drama casts its long shadow even here.

While there is no escaping the shadow of prejudice cast by the Oberammergau play, there is at least some dramatic relief in our own backyard.

*Johannes Reuchlin and the Talmud*, written by Basya Hunter and produced by the students and staff of St.

Michael's College School, is a play that Jewish survivors could watch. This play, which is being presented this weekend, is an unexpected flicker of hope. Bring flowers if you go.

It is striking that a high school would choose to produce this particular play. It is remarkable that a Catholic high school would dramatize the underside of the church's relationship to the Jews.

*Johannes Reuchlin and the Talmud* deals with a sixteenth-century conflict between a Christian theologian and the church. What is at issue is the theologian's unusual openness to Jews and Jewish learning.

The play will have a real impact for the better — just as the Oberammergau play will have its own impact for the worse. Already the drama has had an effect on the actors. Some of their comments bear repeating:

"Before I got into this play I never thought of the church as being so violent. It was as if, as long as you were a Catholic, it was okay to do anything. And that included putting down the Jews. Power was such a big deal." (Michael McManus, who plays the theologian Reuchlin)

"If you look back at the church at that time you could be ashamed. The church was in a mess. But it's good to know that part of our history for living better in the present." (Catherine Meechan, who plays Reuchlin's wife)

"It's amazing. This play shows that the world hasn't changed at all; in fact, it might be worse. For instance, the Jews still seem to get the worst; look at World War Two.... One thing's for sure. We need more of this." (Michael McManus again)

Amen.

*New Year's Day, 1980*
As the party began, I wondered whether this might be our last New Year's together: Jim has already left Toronto

and others will be going this summer: Luigi is excited about the possibility of working in a poorer parish on the outskirts of Lima. Hopes to work with [liberation theologian] Gustavo Gutiérrez – trying to articulate a theology that is shaped by the questions of the poor. Ann has a scholarship to do research in Germany for a year. Promises to send us lots of smelly sausage! Isabel has a job lined up at a small Catholic college in Appalachia. Mark will be teaching at a seminary out in the Pacific north-west. Promised to send himself if there was another New Year's party. Bill and Susan at least will be in Toronto. He has a hefty job with the Ministry of Culture and Communications. Good thing. He and Susan want to have a big family. I hope I will be finished in time to be back at *Catholic New Times* in the fall. My, how responsible we're all getting!

We made a sort of covenant to try to be together on New Year's Eve. Everyone's delighted at the thought – makes the prospect of parting a little easier. Reasons given for continuing to get together: 1) We like each other (Luigi). 2) We could settle in, settle down. We need to challenge each other to remain true to some of our ideals (Ann). 3) We're in for tough times in the church and we need each other's support (Mark). 4) We will never find friends like this again (Isabel).

My reason had something to do with the load of hate mail I received after my *Toronto Star* column on Oberammergau. Frightened me to think about all that free-floating hatred out there. I'd crumple like paper if this was the only feedback I received. Hannah Arendt is right about the importance of making a distinction between one's private and public worlds. You can take on public roles and take stands on social issues as long as you have some space where you can be yourself – where you can be weak and inconsistent and laugh at it all. There is an affirmation that means more than accolades, an honesty that surpasses criticism. Thank God for my community and my friends.

*March 1980*
I've been noticing this Lent that I've been watching a lot of TV in the evenings — trying to unwind after a day of writing. It struck me that I don't remember a thing about any of the shows — or do I? I'm wondering if I remember the commercials. Recalled Hannah Arendt's definition of propaganda — anything repeated often enough becomes true. Was jolted by the statistic that the average watcher of TV will, by the end of his or her life, have watched three solid years of advertising. I'm sure I've been assimilating a whole value system in which people are consumed as they consume many things. This is much more sophisticated and seductive than the Nazi propaganda. I might reject the notion of a master race but I am being exposed constantly to the ideal of the beautiful people.

### ROMERO AND THE REALITY OF THE CROSS
(TS, April 5, 1980)

In our society, Easter is in danger of becoming utterly trivial. One has only to flip through the pages of *Vogue*, *Glamour*, or *Flare* to see the warning signs. Observe the cross-shaped earrings which are the "lovely accessories" of the latest designer fashions. Notice the ultimate macho image: one hairy chest accentuated by a gold crucifix worn about the neck. The cross has become nice'n'easy to wear.

The recent murder of Archbishop Oscar Romero of El Salvador calls us back to the stark reality of the cross. His life and death call us to enter into the holy days of Easter in a more than superficial way.

For a long time Oscar Romero was a Holy Thursday person. He was a priest. Day after day, year after year, he celebrated the Eucharist in memory of the Last Supper of Jesus. Time and again he repeated the words "This is my body which will be given up for you."

But while Oscar Romero was concerned with the souls of his people, he didn't concern himself greatly with their bodies. His task, he felt, was to nourish his flock through the Word and Sacrament. And while the majority of his people sank into more abject poverty, Oscar Romero rose in prominence in the church. He became an archbishop and wore a gold cross about his neck. No one thought of crucifying him then.

Then one day, when he was past fifty, Oscar Romero saw the cross that was crushing his people. He saw the burden of poverty that had been laid upon their backs by other human beings. He saw the nails of injustice that had driven despair deep into their lives. He who had spent hours praying before the image of the dying Jesus now turned to the Christ who was suffering in his brothers and sisters in El Salvador.

Oscar Romero embraced the real cross of the poor. He became a Good Friday person.

Why did this older archbishop step out to help carry the cross of the poor? Not because of a new theology or an ideology but because of the example of another older priest.

Rutilio Grande, a Jesuit whose only "crime" seems to have been his choice to live with the poor, was murdered. It was then that Oscar Romero's eyes were opened to the dark cloud of injustice that had covered El Salvador for decades. It was a darkness that could not be relieved by lighting vigil lamps in the cathedral.

Oscar Romero began to speak against the manmade darkness of the social system in El Salvador. The fire of his spirit became a small flickering light of human hope. The words he spoke against violence and injustice ignited the people with a revolutionary sense of dignity. They could believe that they were more than peasants — they were sons and daughters of God.

In kindling this light in the darkness, Oscar Romero became a Holy Saturday person. In extending his arms to the powerless he became a sign of redemptive love — a real sign of the cross.

Oscar Romero's life stands in judgement over those of us who would want to stay at Holy Thursday. He reminds us that our memory of Jesus remains unreal if we do not embrace the reality of his cross today. However, Oscar Romero's life also stands in judgement over those of us who stay with the despair of Good Friday. He bears witness to the fragile light that emerges with Holy Saturday.

Oscar Romero's light of hope shone forth from a most unlikely place — from the hierarchy of the Roman Catholic Church. That is a sign of hope for all of us. It suggests that the reality of the cross may yet be embraced in the obscure recesses of our hearts and the opaque forms of our institutions.

It would be easy to dismiss the dramatic example of Oscar Romero as irrelevant to our daily reality here. That is the problem. Many of us move about in a dull grey haze most of the time. The weather in Toronto can become a state of mind.

The example of Oscar Romero calls us to acknowledge the darkness that is within us and around us. His life challenges us to turn off our artificial lights, to put away our cosmetics that glitter and glow in the dark. Then, perhaps, the small and real lights of Holy Saturday will begin to flicker.

*April 1980*

Almost everything is done on the thesis that can be done. But I keep on failing the German exam. I've never failed an exam before, and I've been using German in my research for years. It's a total emotional block that I can't seem to get over. Every time I sit down to the exam I start to see all the memos written in German, orders for the transportation of Jews across Europe. It frightens me how deeply this has taken hold of my subconscious. Somehow I think I need to acknowledge that the Nazis aren't just out there, they're in me, in my darkness. Sometimes I feel my hold on sanity is tenuous at best.

A STORY OF HOPE BEYOND DEPRESSION

(TS, May 3, 1980)

William Kurelek's recently published autobiography may well become a classic of Canadian spirituality. *Someone with Me* describes a personal journey which challenges us to examine many of our notions of mental illness and mental health.

Some have called the autobiography of this famous Canadian painter a depressing account. I believe it is a testament of hope.

Kurelek's autobiography has none of the high drama of spiritual classics such as Augustine's *Confessions* or Thomas Merton's *Seven Storey Mountain*. It is a muted story told in a self-deprecating manner. In that sense it is an eminently Canadian story.

Kurelek's journey did not lead from a life of wanton pleasure but rather from a life of chronic depression. His journey took him from the stern environment of a Ukrainian family on the Prairies, through a lumber camp and the Ontario College of Art, and onto the roads of Mexico and the United States.

The most significant stopping-place along Kurelek's way was a four-year stay in a mental institution in England. He was not forced to live with emotional and social misfits. He chose to do so. Why? Because he had a desperate desire to be cured of the depressing sense of inferiority which continually plunged him into despair.

Some may see Kurelek's stay in a mental institution as a sign of his mental illness. Other may see his desire for mental health as already a sign of healthiness. Kurelek himself later saw his desire to be cured as a sign that "Someone" was with him in his journey. Unlike so many, Kurelek neither denied his mental illness nor fatalistically accepted it.

Kurelek was not cured by the battalion of eminent English psychotherapists who sought to treat his illness. He was shocked out of his depression—by electricity and by the personal concern of a therapist who was a Catholic. He was not cured but at least he was no longer immune to life.

After his release, this self-professed atheist wended his way slowly and thoughtfully towards Christianity. No flashes of light, no spiritual shocks, accompanied his conversion to Roman Catholicism. He was not completely cured by his new-found faith but he was "in a quiet way a happier, more glad-to-be-alive person."

This journey had what Kurelek called "a happy ending". On his return to Toronto, the Isaacs Gallery exhibited some of his paintings. Kurelek's reputation was quickly established. He also met his future wife at the Catholic Information Centre.

Kurelek's story challenges those of us who think we can be cured by psychiatry alone. However, it also challenges those of us who believe we can be cured by faith alone. It offers the hope of recovery to those who are depressed or emotionally disturbed. "Not only is it possible for them to recover," he says, "it is possible to take advantage of and put to work the suffering they are going through."

However, it would seem that Kurelek did not hope for a total recovery or complete mental health. At some point he seems to have accepted his limited portion of physical and mental health and said it was "enough" to go on. At this point his art became more than a means of self-expression. It became an expression of his concern about the illnesses of our contemporary society. His art reflected a passionate social concern about the well-being of our country and our world.

Kurelek's example should call us to question the self-centred obsession with physical and psychological "wellness" which is prevalent today. He did not share the secular belief in the salvific myth of total health.

Kurelek did not passively accept his mental illness. However, he did accept the limits of his own psychic growth. Thus he has trodden the path of the relatively happy life which is open to us when we are well "enough" to care for the well-being of others.

"There is Someone with me and always has been. And He has asked me to get up because there is work to be done."

*May 1980*

I had been up all night putting in the final corrections on the thesis. Then some of the people from my community and the thesis group helped me run off the copies and carry them over to the philosophy department—just in time to meet the deadline. Then we fled. Went over to the Brunswick House to celebrate—the place where we had concluded many classes together.

I guess we were a little raucous because the waitress

came over and asked us what was going on. She was quite a fixture at the Brunswick House and I had thought she was a tough old babe — with her big buttressed-up boobs and straw-yellow hair. Someone told her what the occasion was. "Oh, I know what that means," she said, "I just had a daughter graduate from nursing school." Ten minutes later she returned with a big cake, on the house, saying, "Congratulations."

I couldn't help it. I started to cry. It was such a small and genuine act of kindness. It was something my soul longed for, without knowing it, after all the months of exposure to the depths of cruelty. It must have been so for the Jews. How much one small act of kindness could have meant.

### A SERMON IN STONE
### (TS, July 26, 1980)

CHARTRES, FRANCE — They don't make cathedrals like they used to. Perhaps that is why it is so difficult for so many to imagine the church as something more than a building.

This thought came to me as I sat on the steps of the cathedral in Chartres. It was a welcome pause — and a provoking thought — at the beginning of a long business trip in Europe.

Over the centuries, poets and writers have attempted to describe the beauty and grace of this great medieval cathedral. I too was amazed by this monumental hymn in stone and stained glass. Yet I must admit that I was even more fascinated by the process by which this magnificent edifice took shape.

It is a process of building that bears repeating today.

In a few brief paragraphs my trusty guidebook sketched

out the lines of the long history of the building of the cathedral of Chartres. It was a process that lasted for more than a hundred years, and many of the early efforts were destroyed by fire. The catastrophic fire of 1194 would have left most of us contemporary would-be builders in a state of total "burn-out". Yet this trial by fire only served to inflame the zeal for this building for another thirty years.

The people of that time and place followed the example of their bishop, who had turned over his income to resurrect the project. Farmers sold their lands to contribute to the cathedral — a young man donated the precious necklace he had bought for his fiancée. But the people gave much more than their money. They gave of themselves — of their time and their labour. The chronicles of that time tell of the enthusiasm with which teams of volunteers pulled the wagons loaded with stone from the quarries some distance from the village. It was considered a privilege to draw the loads of stone and the volunteers came from all social classes — lords and ladies, the bourgeois, and the peasants. The only point of discrimination was that the honour was reserved for those who had confessed their sins and had pardoned their enemies.

From all over France, skilled artisans came to help in building the cathedral. Generations of families participated in this task. The stained-glass windows give us a glimpse of the society which gave rise to such a building: kings, bishops, money-changers, blacksmiths, wine merchants....

In the process of building there were petty squabbles and theological disputes among the various groups involved. Yet the building continued.

In spite of all the historical accounts of that time, we have no record of the name of the master architect of the cathedral. We know only that it was built by thousands of unnamed workers and artists over generations. Their satisfaction lay, not in the recognition of their individual achievements, but rather in the awareness that together they were building something beautiful for God.

By comparison, the building of a cathedral today is a rather perfunctory affair: the clergy plan, the people pay, and a construction firm builds. With so little investment of self on the part of the people, one wonders if such cathedrals would ever be rebuilt if they went up in smoke.

However, Chartres is a challenge to us to think about much more than just the construction of our cathedrals. It is a challenge to Christians to rediscover the kind of common purpose which can be a focal point for our social life.

Chartres also stands as evidence that such a vision cannot be constructed by a few master builders. This kind of vision can only be realized through the participation of many. Furthermore, Chartres gives us a glimpse of how a compelling vision of faith can encompass the petty squabbles, social frictions, and theological disputes that arise from such participation.

Daydreams on a hot summer afternoon? But Chartres must have seemed like an impossible dream some summer afternoons in the twelfth century.

*August 1980*
The rumour in Rome is that the conservatives are fully in charge of the Vatican once more. Religious communities are feeling the heat as they are asked to submit their constitutions for review; liberation theologians from Latin America are being censured.

I think back to the cathedral of Chartres which was so long in the building. My generation doesn't have any sense of the revolutionary virtue of patience. If we don't succeed in a year or two we are tempted to give up. And most of what we hope for probably won't be realized in our lifetime. The question is whether we can struggle for something that may only be achieved by another generation. Are we in it for the long haul?

YOU CAN'T COUNT ON THE FEW GOOD PEOPLE
(TS, Sept. 20, 1980)

An audience of 1,500 stood and gave a prolonged ovation to three people you would hardly notice in a crowd.

As I was clapping in the midst of that crowd, I realized that tears had started rolling down my cheeks. I started to brush the tears away until I noticed that there were few dry eyes around me.

We were standing and clapping for three old Dutch immigrants who were being awarded the Medal of the Just by Yad Vashem museum, the Israeli government's memorial to the victims of the Holocaust. This award is reserved for those "righteous gentiles" who, at the risk of their own lives, helped Jews during the time of the Third Reich. The ceremony took place at Beth Tzedec synagogue at the end of August.

All the little embers of hope were stirred in my soul when I saw these three Christians come forth to receive their award. They seemed like three flickering vigil lights who had kept the churches from becoming cold, silent, and dark tombs.

While the actions of these "righteous gentiles" give one cause to hope, the facts of those dark times call a Christian to open repentance: most Christians remained silent bystanders as their Jewish neighbours were dragged away. Twenty per cent of the Nazi SS elite were practising Christians. The Vatican negotiated a concordate with Hitler which is still in effect with the present government of Germany.

Pius XII never made an official statement against the atrocities of the Nazis — even when he knew what was happening in the gas chambers — even when the Jews of his own diocese were being rounded up. We know that the Pope helped to shelter a few Jews, but we also know that an incisive statement would have made all the difference in the world to more than a few.

When the Bishop of Münster issued a pastoral letter attacking the murder of the mentally retarded, the Nazis stopped.

Such Christian complicity has deep roots in the anti-Semitism of the churches. This anti-Semitism has been a constant source of anguish for the Jewish people. It has also distorted the gospel message and sapped the vitality of the churches. Yet this dark chapter in the history of the church is not absolutely conclusive because of the example of a few good people such as the three honoured at Beth Tzedec. I was struck by how ordinary these people were.

It is important to ask why these ordinary people aided their fellow human beings at the risk of their own lives. Why did they respond like the good Samaritan when so many others had passed by those who had been abandoned to death? If we knew the answer to that question, the world could be very different from what it is.

Reflecting on the ceremony in honour of the three "righteous gentiles", I realize that there is a profound ambiguity involved in awarding the Medal of the Just. Jozia de Krijger and Ulfert and Margaret Vanderwal were honoured because they were exceptions to a rule of indifference and hatred. In praising their exceptional actions, one is forced to face that rule.

The tragedy of the Holocaust is that the Jewish people were placed in a situation where they were reduced to depending on the goodness of a few good people. As a result, a few Jews were rescued but the vast majority perished. There were simply not enough good people to go around.

The lesson to be learned from this is that we must prevent another situation in which any group is forced to depend only on goodness, pity, and compassion.

What the Jews at that time needed, and what they and many marginal groups need today, is a political and social guarantee of their human rights. To ensure such a guarantee we must develop the attitude of respect which is due to those who are our equals.

We, as Christians, cannot pride ourselves on the goodness of a few if we have not helped to prevent a situation of injustice in which only a few can survive.

A COMMUNITY OF CONCERN
(TS, Oct. 18, 1980)

I am concerned that we are becoming too familiar with killing.

This concern crystallized for me as I read a shocking study which was released by the American Academy of Pediatricians in 1971. According to these statistics, by the time a child reaches the age of fourteen, he or she will have seen 18,000 people "killed" on TV.

This kind of familiarity with killing breeds neither contempt nor concern — it breeds boredom. This kind of familiarity with thousands of make-believe killings tends to make the nightly news of murder and atrocity somewhat unreal. Little wonder that our reaction to Knowlton Nash's nightly litany of the number of people who have been killed becomes confused. We don't know whether to shed a tear, switch channels, or hope for the commercial.

Pity the people who come to us pleading the cause of those who have been killed in one of the slaughterhouses of our world — Cambodia, Uganda, El Salvador, Guatemala.... They come pleading through the media, through humanitarian and church organizations — and they are stunned by the general indifference here to the fate of other human beings.

In various ways, we are given the facts about those who have been tortured and killed in far-away countries. But for those of us who have seen far more than 18,000 killings on TV, it is all too easy to turn off the reality of what is being said.

The news that twenty-four people have been gunned down in one day in El Salvador merits little mention on our evening news. Yet for the mother of one of the murdered men — that son was the whole world for her. Who would dare to indulge in body-count politics in the presence of that mother?

No doubt many of us would respond with compassion and indignation if we were in the presence of the mother of that dead son. But we are here in our armchairs watching TV, and the reality of that murdered son becomes just another of thousands of killings, make-believe or real.

It is indeed a challenge to remain human when one becomes so familiar with killing. On the one hand, we may be tempted to relegate all the killings on TV to dramatic or statistical unreality. Therein lies the way of ultimate indifference. On the other hand, we may be tempted to confront the news of all the real killings in our world. Therein lies the way of madness. Is there any other way?

I want to describe one simple way which has enabled me to resist the increasing trivialization of life and death. I do so with some hesitancy, because it is rather personal. However, it is a way which has enabled me to respond to the realities of our world with a certain peace and purposefulness. It may be helpful to someone else.

When I was little I was encouraged to pray for my family and friends before I went to bed: "God bless Mommy and Daddy and my brother and sister...."

In the past few years, I have reclaimed that prayer as a political and religious activity. At night, I pray for my extended family — for my community of concern composed of people from various troubled areas of the world. I do not pray for countries, or classes, or races, but for real people.

For example: every evening I remember Alicia Theresa Israel, a young lawyer who was working in a human rights organization in Buenos Aires until she disappeared into the black hole of the Argentinian concentration-camp system. She used to write children's stories in her spare time. The military junta of Argentina would like us to forget about people like Alicia Israel. My prayer is the beginning of an act of resistance against such forgetfulness.

In my community of concern there is a little Cambodian boy, a priest from Guatemala, a dissident from Russia, and others. These people are more than statistical figures for me. Their lives and deaths are more than make-believe. Because of them, I am not reduced to a state of indifference or paralysis by the evening news. Because of them, I do what I can.

THE EVENT OF THE HOLOCAUST AND THE
PHILOSOPHICAL REFLECTIONS OF HANNAH ARENDT*

At the outset I want to acknowledge what may negatively be termed my "biases" and what may positively be termed

* From the Introduction of a Ph.D. Thesis

"my convictions". It is my conviction that a philosophical confrontation with the Holocaust should not be avoided even at the expense of conventional philosophical clarity. It is also my conviction that, in the end, one cannot avoid making some decision about, some response to, the Holocaust. If one confronts the Holocaust with integrity, one will have to move beyond philosophizing. Paradoxically, that movement may help to reinstate the integrity of the philosophical enterprise.

I am still in the process of confronting the Holocaust. Because I was born after that event I am, for better or worse, one whom Arendt would call a "spectator".

However, I am convinced that the Holocaust is a part of my past which can be ignored only at my own, and others', peril. Because my own confrontation continues to deepen, I continue to live, somewhat tensely, between half-formed questions and failing answers, between philosophical reflection and personal response. I have neither arrived at insight, nor been reduced to silence. While I am able to discuss another's confrontation with the Holocaust, I am not yet able to speak about my own.

Even as I was writing this essay I struggled to find the words and approach which were appropriate, not only to Arendt, but to the event of the Holocaust itself. I was aware of the predicament which has been so well described by Terrence Des Pres:

> To write about terrible things in a neutral tone or with descriptions barren of subjective response tends to generate an irony so virulent as to end in either cynicism or despair. On the other hand, to allow feeling much play when speaking of atrocity is to border on hysteria and reduce the agony of millions to a moment of self-indulgence.

I doubt if either Arendt or I have resolved that predicament with total success. I also doubt whether the format
of a Ph.D. thesis can allow one to convey the full weight
of the problematic which the Holocaust places not only
on the human mind but also on the human heart and soul.

These convictions and these doubts continue. Conse-
quently, in this essay, my words are muted and my inten-
tions limited.

### October 1980

My thesis defence was like nothing I could have imagined.
It had passed through all the readers and through Emil
Fackenheim without a hitch. All the signs were for clear
sailing.

But I knew something was wrong when I was kept
waiting outside the examination room for what seemed
like for ever. What was the problem? I learned the next
day that Emil Fackenheim was raking the other professors
over the coals — because they couldn't possibly understand
what the Holocaust was about.

Then I went in. The questions were polite, perfunctory,
strained. Then it was Emil's turn. His opening question:
"Where was the church in all of this? Why didn't the Pope
say anything?"

I was taken aback at having been put in a position of
defending the Vatican. Emil knew how critical I have been
of the Vatican's silence. I wanted to reach out and say,
"It's me, remember, Mary Jo. We've celebrated Passover
together at your house."

But it wasn't me. I was only a Roman Catholic. And
this wasn't about a philosophy thesis. This was about
religion and politics.

I just kept repeating, "I don't know. I don't know."
Over and over until it was over.

Apparently, after I left, Emil apologized to the other

professors, as he did to me later. "I don't know what happened," he said. "I've never done that before at a defence."

I knew what had happened. I had wanted so much to defend the small but certain clarity I had come to in writing the thesis. But I was asked to defend what I couldn't defend. It wasn't so outrageous to be put on the defensive. I have shared in the blessings of this church so I have to carry the burden of its past as well.

At least I wasn't asked to defend God. It is not the God I would have chosen. I would want Someone more pure, less muddied by history. Yet this is the real God, the God who has entered into our history. We cannot abandon this real God without abandoning the reality of our own human history. Martin Buber's lines ring true: "We cannot cleanse the word 'God' and we cannot make it whole; but, defiled and mutilated as it is, we can raise it from the ground and set it over an hour of great care."

# III

*A Certain Clarity*

*November 1980*
No sooner had I returned to *Catholic New Times* than I
was tossed the hottest potato I have ever had to deal with.
"A very highly placed source" phoned and asked to have
lunch in a very discreet, tucked-away little restaurant.
There he told me that the cardinal was cutting back the
Sharelife funds to the third world but was not saying so
publicly. The source said that this was partly because of
the cardinal's irritation over some of the justice stands
that the independently run Canadian Catholic Organization for Development and Peace (CCODP) had taken —
particularly its decision to withdraw its account from the
Royal Bank because of that bank's position on apartheid.
"Check out the Sharelife board of directors," said the
source, "and you'll see who's influencing the cardinal on
this decision." The source also said he'd heard rumours
that the Vatican wanted all the money for the third world
to go first to the Vatican bank. This would allow the
Vatican to bottleneck the money and earn some interest

on it in order to pay off the Vatican debts; it would also allow the Vatican to control the distribution of the funds in the third world.

I could hardly believe my ears. It sounded like something we could, must take on. It could sink us, though — this was heavy stuff. I wished it were an issue I was more prepared to deal with — apartheid has not been on my front burner. But you don't always choose the issues, sometimes they choose you. We will go with this — wherever it takes us.

Have spent weeks in the Business section of the Metro Toronto Library poring over volumes of information about who owns what in the corporate world. All my training in research is coming in handy, in ways I hadn't expected. This much is clear: many of the honorary directors of Sharelife are directly or indirectly (through interlocking directorships) linked to the Royal Bank and to companies that do business in South Africa, military business. But I can't yet prove a direct link between their interests and the cardinal's decision to cut back the funds to Development and Peace.

These men are probably all rather nice people.

This issue is consuming all my time. The day-to-day operation of the paper is suffering. We're all overloaded, snapping at each other. We really don't have the human resources to take on something like this. But how can we not?

THE SHADOW OF RACISM IN CANADA
(CNT, Nov. 16, 1980)

TORONTO — The Canadian Council of Churches has emerged as a reluctant prophet in the struggle against racism in Canada.

The churches have taken an official stance which has disturbed those Canadians who presume that racism is a distant problem in South Africa or south of the border. Even concerned Christians, who would never identify with Archie Bunker, are perturbed by the churches' claim that there is a racist society north of the forty-ninth parallel.

The fall marks the end of a period of intense ferment during which the Canadian Council of Churches has tried to come to grips with the seeds of racism in this society. A year-long process of prayer and reflection, involving groups across the country, crystallized in the publication last spring of a report entitled "Racism in Canada".

The churches have identified the native peoples as the prime, although not the only, target of racism in this country. According to the churches, the treatment of native peoples today reflects the "original sin" of Canada. The report, commissioned by the Taskforce on Racism, elaborates on the ways the exploitation of the native peoples since the time of the first explorers has become embedded in the structures of this society.

"Racism in Canada" documents an important shift in the churches' approach to the racism in their own backyard. Racism is no longer seen as the ugly quality of certain fanatical groups or as a moment of meanness between individuals. Racism is now seen as a pervasive characteristic of the pattern of relationships inherent in the Canadian socio-economic system.

A native woman has described the made-in-Canada brand of racism in this way: "Racism is a shadow — a travelling companion who's only dead when you're sleeping. No! Even sleep is interrupted."

At both the local and national levels, the Canadian Council of Churches is being questioned on its involvement with the issue of racism. Doesn't the role of the churches lie elsewhere? Bob Haverluck, the chairperson of the Taskforce on Racism in Saskatchewan, has argued eloquently against the view that religion has only to do with things spiritual. "The God of those who maintain this perspective," he says, "becomes a blind dove confined to the constricted bird cage of their own insides, while they go about seeking material possessions with a frenzy."

Yet it would seem that the churches are not content merely to shake their fingers at the evils of racism in this society. The churches have started to beat their breasts about the racism which is to be found in their own attitudes and structures.

Some church representatives are quick to point out that the churches have been historically involved in the oppression of the native peoples. "Racism in Canada" describes the way the early missionaries conveyed to the native peoples not only the gospel but the paternalistic attitude of a white society as well. Well-meaning Christians were often unwitting instruments in the destruction of the fabric of native cultures and societies.

Stan McKay has spoken bitterly about the forms of paternalistic racism which continue to exist, albeit subtly, within the churches. As someone who is both a native and the United Church minister in Koostatak, Manitoba, McKay criticizes the "liberal guilt" which he feels motivates much of the churches' response to his people. "Natives are thought of as underprivileged children, not as the victims of racism."

The churches have also been warned about the blind spot in their own struggle with the shadow of racism. At the National Consultation on Racism held in Winnipeg last April, Robert Vachon spoke about the racist streak in the churches' own approach to racism.

Vachon, director of the Montreal cross-cultural Centre-Monchanin, noted that the cultural blinkers of the churches make them "generally unable to look at other peoples and cultures except as a problem to be solved or an emptiness to be filled." Thus, he said, the churches refer to the "needy", the "poor", the "underdeveloped", the "minorities", and the "oppressed". These people are always viewed as without something: without education, without jobs, without social skills, and without power. "We end up defining them and their condition exclusively by what we believe they lack rather than by what they truly are, thus denying them their original and unique identity."

*December 1980*
Still pursuing the story of the cutback to the Development and Peace funds. On November 20 and December 9 I interviewed Paul Robinson, the head of Sharelife. He was very friendly. He tried to evade my simple questions through flattery and folksy ways. Does he really think that's all it takes? He tried desperately to present himself as someone who was an intimate of cardinals, bishops, and the corporate elite—as well as being a champion of the poor. He also portrayed the cardinal as being very palsy-walsy with the corporate types, and definitely indicated that they had conversed about South Africa several times.

When I pointed out that the cutback to Development and Peace was carefully obscured by the Sharelife literature, Robinson said, "We said there would be one bright person who would pick it up as they read it." I wouldn't have picked it up if it weren't for our source.

Reviewing the transcripts of the tape, I decided not to print the interview. The indiscretions and exaggerations made it all of dubious value. Never discount the stupidity factor! Will phone Bishop Wall to ask him to clarify the transcripts.

FOUR AMERICAN NUNS
(TS, Dec. 13, 1980)

I had planned to write something joyful, something innocent and heartfelt, for Christmas; then I heard the shocking news of the rape and murder of four Roman Catholic
missionaries in El Salvador. That event dictated otherwise.

To date, the evidence suggests that these four American
women were murdered by government security forces.
Their deaths increase the toll of more than 8,000 lives
which have been taken in the violent conflict in El
Salvador.

In the struggle between rich and poor, between the
military, the government, and the people, many church
workers have made "an option for the poor".

Of the four women who were murdered, two were Maryknoll sisters—Sister Ita Ford and Sister Maura Clarke. I
did not know them personally, but I know whereof they
come. I have been closely associated with people from
Maryknoll over the years. Maryknoll is an American mission society with priests, sisters, and lay members. I have
studied with Maryknollers, worked with them, and lived
in their communities.

A few summers ago, in Boston, I taught philosophy to
a group of young men and women who were training to
become Maryknoll missionaries. These students were very
ordinary young people—as American as apple pie. They
came from small towns in New England, in the Midwest,
or, like Ita Ford and Maura Clarke, from closely knit
neighbourhoods in larger cities. They had grown up on
football games and parish bazaars. They represented all
that is best in small-town America. Every one of them had
learned the lessons of their own nation's history well. They
were proud of their origins in a revolution against English

tyranny. They felt the ideals of democracy were worth fighting for — ideals of liberty, equality, and fraternity. It was their dedication to these ideals which made them all the more aware of the gap between those ideals and some of the realities of the contemporary republic.

This awareness increased when these young people went overseas. In their letters they wrote about their growing love and respect for people of a different language and culture. They also described their terrible realization that the democratically elected American government was propping up dictators or military juntas which denied the basic rights of other peoples. The security of American democracy at home was being bought at the price of tyranny abroad.

When these young people went to the third world and upheld the American ideal that all people are created free and equal, when they preached the revolutionary good news that each person is created in the image of God, they were loosely labelled "leftists" or "Commies".

Two weeks before Ita Ford and Maura Clarke were murdered, a warning was placed on the door of their residence. It read: "In this house are Communists." The message ended with the drawing of a knife plunged into a skull dripping blood.

The word "Communist" is so inflammatory that it makes most Americans, and indeed most Catholics, see red. And they are blinded to some significant realities. The fear of Communism has often made well-intentioned democrats and Christians unfortunate bedfellows with Fascist forms of government. Such liaisons today are corrupting the soul of the American people at home and are perverting the spirit of the gospel.

It is tragic that these two women were probably murdered with weapons supplied by the American government. It is shameful that almost all the bishops in El

Salvador have refused to come to the defence of church workers who, like the two Maryknoll sisters, have cast their lot with the poor.

These missionaries were not Communists. They were legitimate children of the American revolution, and daughters of a church built on the blood of martyrs.

### New Year's Day, 1981

Talked a lot last night about the four American women who had been raped and killed. It wasn't a sad conversation, though. I think we feel encouraged and challenged by these women—how they lived and how they died says it all. I had the thought that they were probably very much like Ann and Isabel—everything best in America struggling against everything worst in it. These four women were for real—a welcome change from all the cutesy nun images on TV or the rigid frigid stereotypes in habits. Bill had composed a song in honour of the women which Susan sang: "Future generations will call you blessed." It was rather poignant—especially since Susan had another miscarriage in the fall.

Ann (from Germany) and Luigi (from Peru) both sent letters to be shared at the gathering. Ann says that what happened in El Salvador has made her proud to be an American nun. Says she is underwhelmed by the church scene in Germany. "There is a lot more substantial and creative thinking going on in North America. It's about time we stopped looking to Europe for the answers." Luigi's letter was predictably humorous. "How I miss our beautiful bourgeois parties. Will you be having Perrier and quiche?!!" He said the people of his parish have been lighting candles in front of the pictures of the four American women—"women of light, women of God".

Somehow these women have given me more emotional clarity about the Sharelife issue. I must keep my eyes focused on the people who will be affected by the financial cutbacks. Luigi wrote about how the construction of a filtration system (paid for by Development and Peace) has meant clean water for the neighbourhood, the difference between life and death for some children in his parish. The survival of *Catholic New Times* must be a secondary consideration. These four women knew there was no middle ground — you are either for the poor or against them.

We toasted Ann and Luigi with a jug of hooch that Isabel brought up from Appalachia. The slower pace, the simpler life, seems to be agreeing with her. Modest. Isabel is so much more gentle in her expectations than the rest of us. Loves seeing her students learn, enjoys visiting the people in the "hollers". She's as clear on the issues as any of us but seems less driven by them. And Mark seems more content now that he's teaching the seminarians. Something about the priesthood started coming alive for him when he was really called upon to share it with others. Says he's joined a peace group protesting at the nearby Strategic Air Command base. He had some words of wisdom for me: "Don't worry about polishing every story. In two weeks, someone will be using the paper to wrap up their soggy garbage!" Ahem.

### SOLIDARITY AS A HABIT OF BEING
(CNT, Jan. 18, 1981)

You might expect a man who is passionately concerned about political prisoners to have a tortured look. You might expect a former political prisoner to have a haunted, hunted look.

Pepe (José) Zalaquett, the international chairman of Amnesty International, shatters these expectations when he greets you with a smile that flashes freedom from ear to ear. That smile is the measure of the man.

One wonders who would want to imprison this gentle and generous man. One understands immediately why he is the head of an international movement which has been awarded the Nobel Prize for Peace because of its tenacious struggle in the battle for human rights: sincerity beyond sentiment, competence beyond efficiency, and humour deeper than realism.

His visit to Canada coincided with the recent release of the "Amnesty International Report 1980", a wide-ranging account of challenges to human rights in 110 nations.

A Chilean lawyer, Pepe Zalaquett was expelled by the military regime of Pinochet. Although he claims no formal membership in any church, he was closely involved with the Catholic church in Chile through organizations for justice.

"I'm not a pious person," he says with a certain whimsy, "and I'm rather agnostic about classical theological questions." Nevertheless, he claims to be utterly convinced about "the contribution of Christianity to the common pool of human values such as love and the dignity of the human person."

For this faithful human being, love has more to do with solidarity than with soap operas. "Solidarity is love in a real social, historical, and structural context." With Pepe Zalaquett solidarity has evidently become a habit of being.

On the subject of solidarity, he knows whereof he speaks.

After the destruction of the democratically elected government of Salvador Allende in 1973, many people in Chile turned to the churches as the last haven of human rights. Zalaquett reminisces: "The churches were the only institutions which could act with certain protections. Everyone knocked at the doors of the churches."

He joined the efforts of the churches to salvage human rights in Chile "because it was the only meaningful thing I could do as a lawyer." The ecumenically based Peace Committee grew to a legal and human rights department involving about seventy-five lawyers as well as doctors, religious, and priests throughout the country.

Not to his surprise, Zalaquett was arrested in 1975, along with a number of other lawyers. "We knew what we were getting into." At the same time, the Pinochet regime demanded that the cardinal dissolve the Peace Committee. He complied with the order, and promptly re-established the organization under another name — that of the now famous Vicariate of Solidarity.

Zalaquett does not wear his three months in prison on his sleeve. "So many others suffered so much more," he says quite simply. "I was neither tortured nor killed."

It was Amnesty International that opened the door of the cell that seemed closed to justice and compassion. Throughout the world, small groups of ordinary people wrote letters demanding Zalaquett's release. The military could not easily consign him to a hole of oblivion and add him to the growing list of the "disappeared".

He was expelled instead. But there was a price to pay for that relatively lenient "sentence". Left behind were his wife and two daughters. "It's difficult for me to talk about. You see, I cannot be part of their growing up." It is not something he wants to dwell on.

He prefers to speak of the "absolute privilege" of working to free those who have been imprisoned for their beliefs, colour, sex, ethnic origin, religion, or language — those who have neither used nor advocated violence. His community of concern extends to the victims of the many "isms" that trample on human rights.

Zalaquett has been impressed by the theological reflection in Latin America and speaks with obvious familiarity about its evolution from a theology of liberation to a theology of captivity. "There are many theologies of liberation and many stages of evolution. In the earliest writings there was a natural degree of immaturity. Now, after many years of defeat and suffering, theologians are tending to speak of captivity as a period in the same struggle. And in that captivity they are speaking of community and hope."

In a time of captivity, Pepe Zalaquett is one of the many small, steady lights of the human spirit.

*January 1981*
Three of us from the newspaper went to see Bishop Leonard Wall with the research I had done and the transcripts of the interviews with Paul Robinson. We told him what we had learned about the corporate connections of the men on the Sharelife board and wondered whether the bishops had considered this in their appointments. We also told the bishop about the indiscretions of Paul Robinson and wondered why such a man had been given a position of such responsibility. We told the bishop that we were aware of the cutbacks to Development and Peace and that we would be making it an issue during the coming fund-raising drives if we did not have a sense that the issues were being addressed.

Bishop Wall smiled slightly and said, "You may be sure that I will bring this to the attention of the highest authorities."

BETWEEN SUSPICION AND SIMPLICITY
(TS, March 9, 1981)

Suspicion is becoming the name of the big game called life.

It is no longer the sole preserve of those with a "suspicious nature" but an acquired habit of many in our culture. It is the undisputed virtue of the tacticians of survival. Slowly, but very surely, we are being introduced into ever more sophisticated levels of suspicion.

- We are told by psychiatrists that our motivations are rarely what they seem to be. And so the long, labyrinthine search for the hidden sources of our psychic responses.
- We are told by sociologists that the institutions of our society are buttressed by unacknowledged ideologies. They introduce, for example, the suspicion that our educational and medical systems may serve the interests of a certain class.
- We are told by feminists that a woman who finds a measure of happiness in this chauvinist society must be "unaware". Such a woman is so oppressed, they say, that she does not even know it.
- We are told by church reformers that many of the official reaffirmations of dogmas are little more than a justification of clerical control.
- We are told by consumers' groups that we are all being seduced on a subliminal level by the advertising industry.
- We are told by politicians that other politicians have a hidden agenda.

The implications seem clear. If we are to survive in this world, we must cultivate a sophisticated suspicion. We must become psychologically aware, socially conscious, and politically astute. The fate worse than death would be to sit in a comfortable pew without knowing that we had been ripped off, put down, emotionally manipulated, sexually stereotyped, and socially oppressed.

In its extreme form, the cult of suspicion finds its paired

opposite in the cult of simplicity. In the face of a culture of complexity, mere consistency exercises considerable charm. Thus we are witnessing the revival of an unquestioning religiosity, of an unblinking allegiance to the political and social groups (of the left or right), and of an unshaken affirmation of traditional family roles.

In my opinion, suspicion and simplicity have become forms of superstition in our sophisticated society. Such suspicion leads to a grinding despair, and such simplicity leads to a reckless optimism. Neither leads to the realism of what I would call faith.

The way of suspicion is the way of those who tear down the idols of ideology and illusion. Yet how often the way stops short of breaking the last idol. We must become suspicious of suspicion itself. The way of simplicity is the way of those who build altars to deities both old and new. For the suspicious, the world within and without becomes a wasteland. For the simple, the world becomes a dreamland.

The way of faith lies between the two contemporary superstitions of suspicion and simplicity. It is in a sense neither, and in a sense both.

It is a way of trust which does not bypass but rather encompasses the suspicions of our society. Faith enables us to travel through the reality of a world which is both less — and more — than it appears to be.


### RESTORING THE IMAGE OF GOD
(CNT, April 26, 1981)

"Never make statements that would not remain credible in the presence of burning children." That is the new principle of doing theology after the Holocaust, according to Rabbi Irving Greenberg, the guest speaker at a recent

Jewish-Christian dialogue in Toronto. Greenberg argues that the response of faith and the task of theology have changed radically since the Hitler era.

He stressed the urgency of faith testifying in the present world through actions rather than through words. When children are burning in a pit, the response of faith is to leap into the pit to save a child rather than to preach about God's love. "That is a statement in itself," he said.

With gentle lucidity, Greenberg suggested that the image of God had been shattered and broken in the Holocaust—because human beings had been shattered and broken. The religious response in the contemporary world is to re-create the image of God — to rehabilitate the image of God in suffering humanity. "The single most important thing is to create an image of God, to point to a human being, to treat a person as unique and of infinite value," he said. This implies, he pointed out, that to take any group—women, blacks, natives—and restore them to dignity is to restore the image of God.

The re-creation of human persons in the image and likeness of God involves giving them the power to become equals, argued Greenberg. However, he noted that both Judaism and Christianity "in the good old days" have tended to glorify powerlessness. In the contemporary world, he said, this glorification can only be a partial truth.

In describing the overwhelming evil of the Holocaust, Greenberg indicated why the crucifixion could no longer be presented only as an idealization of powerlessness. In the Nazi system of mass murder, individual martyrdom was no longer an option. People were herded together into gas chambers so that 10,000 would die a nameless death in twenty-five minutes. Under the overwhelming power of such evil, many cracked and lost a sense of their own humanity. This cracking of humanity continues in the world today.

The lesson of the crucifixion must be relearned in the midst of this experience of powerlessness, said Greenberg. "The lesson of the cross is that even God himself on a cross would have cracked. If God could not take it, neither could any other human being take it. The religious response to the cross today is to give people enough power so that they will not be placed in a position of absolute powerlessness," he said.

To emphasize the reality of the contemporary forms of crucifixion, Greenberg suggested that if Jesus were placed on trial in the Soviet Union he would not be able to defy the authorities as he once did. "Those who have been worked on with mind drugs will end up by confessing their guilt and by acknowledging that the system is right."

The fundamental crisis facing religious people today, he said, is the crisis of human solidarity. Referring to the statistics of the Holocaust, he pointed out that the single most important factor in determining the fate of the victims was the reaction of the bystanders. Where the bystanders protested against the Nazi actions, there were fewer victims. Where there was silence in the face of Nazi activities, there were many victims. "We have to go through our religious traditions and weed out all that creates distance and lack of concern," he said.

HOPE STILL GROWS IN A DESERTED WORLD
(TS, July 25, 1981)

A blank, beige area on the map—that used to be my predominant image of the desert. Now, having lived in the reality of the desert, I know it is the place where we both escape and encounter the reality of our life in the city.

During a five-week stay in Israel this summer, I travelled through the Sinai desert for a few days. Like the other members of the tour group, I was anticipating the heat and the thirst. But none of us was prepared for the stark beauty of the desert.

With the luxury of a full tank of gas and a large container of water, we had the security of journeying into the desert more with fascination than with fear. As we drove along in our open command car, mountains of stone greeted us at every turn. Shifting scenes of rocky grandeur. Silence everywhere. Camels came and went silently over the horizon. A few Bedouin waved silently as we passed. At night we cooked and slept on the sand under the clearest of skies.

I had entered a space which was both foreign and familiar.

There, in the silence, the sun, and the rock, I discovered anew the God of my ancestors in the faith. Like Moses and his people, we were wandering somewhere in a space where the memory of past liberation fades and the hope of future liberation falters. In the in-between space of the desert, one recognizes the stark reality of believers in the world today.

In this desert I sought — and found — a reason to hope in a world which sometimes seems deserted by both God and humanity. My hope did not drop from the heavens — nor did it emerge from conversations with my fellow travellers.

My small hope sprang up with the little green plants in the desert. These shoots of hope, unlike the palm trees in the oases, seem inexplicable. On a face of sheer rock they flash a green wink at those who have accepted the desert's mask of stone. When you see life bursting forth from lifeless stone, you find reasons (perhaps like Moses) to trust in a Creator God. When you see little green plants springing from nowhere, it is easier to believe in a God who creates something out of nothingness.

Our cities today often seem like places of stone — stony faces, stony hearts. Schools, churches, factories, and offices can sometimes seem like monuments to the reality of the stone wall of the status quo.

Yet the experience of the desert can lead the believer back to the city of stone with a small but sure hope. If little green plants can spring up in the desert, then our own hearts of stone may yet change. There is reason to hope that life will burst forth in the cracks and crevices of the institutions of our society. There is reason to wink at our own masks of stone.

*September 1981*

Notes from interview with Adolfo Perez Esquivel, 1980 Nobel Peace Prize winner:

"I was in a torture centre, imprisoned in a small narrow cell without light or sanitary facilities. When they opened the door, letting in the light, I could see many inscriptions on the walls. One day they left the door open a little longer than usual, and when I looked more closely around the cell I saw, on one wall, a big bloodstain. Below it, written by a finger dipped in the blood, it said: '*Dios no mata'* — God does not kill. This is something that has burned into my memory and will be with me for the rest of my life."

PRISONER WITHOUT A NAME,
CELL WITHOUT A NUMBER
(CNT, Sept. 13, 1981)

The publication of Jacobo Timerman's book *Prisoner without a Name, Cell without a Number* is a literary and a political event.

The book is a searing testimony of a witness who spent

thirty months in the dark underworld of Argentina's military system. Written with eloquent restraint, it communicates the silent scream of the 20,000 human beings who have disappeared into the holes of oblivion in that country.

Since its release a few months ago, the book has fanned a storm of controversy in the United States and elsewhere. Supporters of the military junta in Argentina and of the Reagan administration in the States have engaged in an intense effort to discredit the author.

Who is Jacobo Timerman and why are they saying such awful things about him? From 1971 until his arrest, he was the editor and publisher of *La Opinión*, an influential newspaper in Buenos Aires. Although he had written in opposition to left-wing terrorism, after 1976 he became one of the few public opponents of the right-wing terrorism which flourished under General Videla.

In a country where propaganda created the daily fiction of normalcy, he told the truths of fact by publishing the names of those who had disappeared. And neither those facts nor Jacobo Timerman fitted into the ordered universe being constructed by the military. He did not fit, claims Timerman, not only because he was a passionate champion of freedom but also because he was passionately Jewish.

Now he has emerged from a world of the living dead to testify. It is a testimony on behalf of those who may never reappear. "Each time I write or utter words of hope, words of confidence in the definitive triumph of man, I'm fearful—fearful of losing sight of one of those gazes. At night I recount them, recall them, resee them, cleanse them, illumine them."

No—this account is not a hymn of hope. Timerman's rage is not concealed and his mercy knows some bounds. He testifies pointedly against the military junta, against the Jewish leaders in Argentina, and against the silent spectators of it all.

He testifies as one who has seen the naked apes in the undergrowth of his society. In his analysis of that situation, the struggle is not primarily between left and right but rather between civilization and barbarism. His evidence is cogent and persuasive.

From Timerman's perspective, the government of Argentina resembles nothing so much as the Fascist regime of Hitler. While some may dispute the structural parallels Timerman draws, it is difficult to ignore his account of discussions with the military and with his torturers.

In one chilling passage, an Argentinian officer calmly tells Timerman that the enemies of the regime should be exterminated. "All...about twenty thousand people. And their relatives too—they must be eradicated—and also those who remember their names."

One senses that Timerman saw the Fascist face of Argentina most clearly when he saw the contorted faces of his torturers screaming, "Jew!" He is convinced that he was imprisoned more for being a Jew than for being an outspoken journalist.

Amnesty International's 1980 report entitled "Secret Concentration Camps in Argentina" substantiates his claim that the Jews were the objects of particular hatred in the prisons. "Most of those killed were not Jews" writes Timerman, "and if we continue to feel sorry for ourselves as Jews we will end up being hated by the non-Jewish victims, by the families of those priests and nuns who were murdered. But in the solitude of prison, it is so sad to be beaten for being Jewish. There is such despair when they torture you for being Jewish. It seems so humiliating to have been born...."

Yet Timerman says that the physical pain he endured

was not to be compared with the moral suffering inflicted on him by the silence of the Jewish leaders in the country. He compares their silent acquiescence to his fate with the co-operation of the Jewish councils with Hitler's extermination of their own people.

Little wonder, then, that this book has occasioned more than literary reviews. In clearly defining Argentina's government as totalitarian, Timerman has presented a singular indictment of present American foreign policy. UN ambassador Jeane Kirkpatrick has relied on a convenient distinction between authoritarian and totalitarian governments to justify her country's continued support for "merely authoritarian" governments which happen to violate human rights. Try telling Timerman that his government was "merely authoritarian" or "moderately repressive".

Many supporters of the Reagan policy, some of whom happen to be Jewish, have attempted to discredit Timerman by saying that he received funds from leftist sources. The moral obtuseness of these critics is obvious. Even if their charge were true (which I doubt), it would not justify one moment of the inhuman treatment Timerman and thousands of others were subjected to.

Timerman's pen is becoming a sword of division in the Jewish community—raising the question of whether Reagan's support of Israel is being bought at the expense of the human rights of Jews and others elsewhere.

In the end, those who consider Timerman's testimony seriously will have to answer a basic question: has he been enlightened or blinded by his experience as a prisoner without a name in a cell without a number? I think he sees the shadowed world we live in more clearly than most.

*September 1981*
We've written our first editorial on Development and Peace. Dealt only with organizational and policy issues — not yet ready to publish the financial shenanigans. Yet even without this info, the editorial created quite a stir. Lots of letters and phone calls from people concerned about the future of the organization. They'd better be.

*October 14, 1981 (Notes from conference "The Writer and Human Rights")*
Impressed with Eastern bloc writers: Josef Brodsky, Josef Skvorecky, Natalya Gorbanevskaya.

Susan Sontag points out that many North American and Latin American writers have chosen not to criticize the human-rights violations of the Soviet Union because they do not want their criticisms to be used by the American government to justify its present foreign policy. "I have operated on a double standard, like many American writers," she says.

But she has found the testimony of the Eastern Bloc dissidents over the past eight years impossible to ignore. She urges Western writers to abandon the moral compromise of this "double standard" and to work resolutely against becoming politically compromised.

Eduardo Galeano criticizes those who would see writing as a sacred task disconnected from the struggles of others, or as a politically useless effort. Against this pride and false humility, Galeano describes literature as a form of action: "It has no supernatural powers. It has a social function if the readers change."

He invites writers to create images of a more human way of life.... In a situation where human beings are robbed of their dignity, a love story can be profoundly political by "lighting the little fires of memory, identity, and hope." The writer who sparks the imagination and the will to change is giving "more shelter to naked people left outside in intemperate weather" than those who sketch the stereotypes of exploitation.

Galeano is really the first person who has given me a sense of writing as a vocation. "Writing is my way of acting in the world." I think I have been thinking of it as something less than acting in the world. I also think he is right about the importance of love stories, stories of goodness to help people remember their own dignity. I must try to do more of this. It would mean drawing on more of myself.

ORIGINAL SIN
(Editorial, CNT, Nov. 22, 1981)

The proposed Charter of Rights is a tragically flawed document. What was intended to guarantee a just and tolerant society will further entrench a fundamental discrimination against the native peoples.

On Thursday November 5, the aboriginal and treaty rights of the native peoples were dropped from the Charter of Rights. Trudeau claimed that it was a price some premiers had exacted in the process of the historic compromise. Yet that evening the federal government pushed Bill C-48 through its final vote in the House of Commons. Accurately described as the "biggest land grab" in Canadian history, this bill places native land claims at the mercy of the Minister of Energy.

We have gained access to the energy resouces of the north and suffered the loss of our national soul. Foul has become legally fair.

In the face of such flagrant betrayal, the churches must act swiftly and unequivocally in defence of the native peoples' aboriginal and treaty rights.

If there is a political "original sin" which corrupts the history of this country, it is the systematic denial of the rights of our aboriginal people. This sin is prior to the more obvious fratricidal conflict between English and French which characterizes our country. And as long as this "original sin" against the native peoples is embedded in our laws and structures we will remain what we really are — a racist society.

Racism in Canada is subtle but none the less severe. With documents of fine print we paper over the hideous reality of ravaged lives. And smile and smile.

Unless aboriginal and treaty rights are included in the Charter of Rights, it becomes but a flimsy guarantee for us all. The rights of all are potentially in jeopardy as long as the rights of one group are denied.

We need a political act of redemption at this critical moment in our history. Let us call upon God. Call upon one another. Call upon the members of parliament. May they not rest in peace.

*New Year's Day, 1982*

I needed to be at the gathering last night. As my research on the Sharelife cutbacks drags on, I am more tempted to feel cynical about the church. It's not a feeling I like — in myself or others. When I'm with my friends, telling the truth seems like a much more hopeful activity.

Ann tossed out the question "Why do we stay in the church anyway?" Talk about getting to the heart of the matter! Jim said he was more cynical about the government than about the church. Bill agreed. We all have to make our way in some institution or drop out of society altogether. The only question is — which one shows the most promise of reform? Ann, who's just finished her first few months teaching at an ivy-league school on the east coast, said there was very little possibility of reforming academic institutions.

Then Mark began to speak with great conviction and eloquence about the dangerous memory of Jesus that was carried within the flawed structure of the church—a memory that surfaces again and again in history, a memory of holiness and love that makes it possible for us to recognize sin and darkness. "A dangerous memory that erupts unexpectedly into hope—witness Romero, the four women. It's the most important memory we have. Sometimes the church makes it more difficult to remember this Jesus, but it never quite lets us forget him."

It was so still we could hear each other breathing. Then Isabel, tears streaming down her face, leaned forward and said in all sincerity, "Oh Mark, I just love the way you talk." We dissolved in howls of laughter. Bill made a motion that Mark should give a ferverino every New Year's. Seconded by Ann.

Actually, Ann has already helped us answer the question she posed. She's introduced some of us to Bishop Tom Gumbleton, the auxiliary bishop of Detroit. She met him back in the sixties when he was the first bishop to speak out against the war in Vietnam. That was the end of his ecclesiastical career but the beginning of his leadership role in forming the "peace church" in the U.S. The moral clarity of his own life (he lives in a poor inner-city parish) has given us all reason to believe in the church. I'm finding that I don't need big reasons to believe—just real reasons. A few friends, a community, one believable bishop—it seems enough to go on.

The commitment of Mark and Gumbleton to the peace movement has awakened a desire in me to get more involved. The desire draws deeply on the convictions formed by my confrontation with the Holocaust. Now we are facing the final solution of the human race. Everything,

everything depends on living the truth of this moment. There is no middle ground. The times are demanding much of us. The problem is that up until now, too little has been asked of us.

In the midst of all of this, a new little world in the making. Bill and Susan are expecting in the spring. This is the first pregnancy that has gone beyond three months, so there is cause for celebration. If it's a girl, she will be called Ann. If a boy, Christopher.

## SURVIVAL AS A SPIRITUAL RESPONSE
### (CNT, March 21, 1982)

The ground is shifting beneath our feet. Beneath our pedestrian feet, our pilgrim feet, a basic shift is taking place. But our hearts are afraid to feel it, our heads only slowly think it, and our hands do not know what to do with it.

Nuclear nightmares in the day: we can no longer take the earth for granted. Humanity is an endangered species.

We've been losing ground since Hiroshima and Nagasaki. If we think we have something to stand on, perhaps it's because we have buried our heads in the sand.

The possibility of a nuclear holocaust has made all the difference in the world. It is a substantial difference and it demands a different spiritual response.

So many of our spiritual resources were discovered, mined, and refined in another age. Our spiritual tradition is a rich treasure house where one can seek and find — but for how long? When will the walls come tumbling down? It is these questions, imploding in our minds with a nuclear blast, which set us in search of a spirituality for this age.

For a long time, Christians could take the earth for

granted. It was solid ground, the place where people were born and died, where empires rose and fell, where dreams of another world seemed real. Because they could take the world for granted, they could seek the higher and better. The church could preach that there was more to life than just living. Christians were invited to imitate their Master, to sacrifice themselves for the sake of love and truth and liberation. They were called to sacrifice themselves, if need be, to the point of death. The martyr, the saint, the monk, and the missionary were various models of the way of sacrifice for the sake of a higher good.

Yet in this nuclear age, the earth is no longer a sure starting point. Our technology has fashioned a stop-watch and we are able, for the first time, to put an end to the human race.

Once we admit that we are on very shaky ground, many of the distinctions constructed in a more solid time begin to collapse: higher and lower, heaven and earth, the holy and the human.

In a nuclear age, many of the tasks which used to seem lowly and all too human may become holy works. At a time when organized death predominates, simply staying alive may be as religious a response as accepting death. When the nuclear idols demand holocaust and burnt offerings, the greater good may be to refuse to sacrifice human life. The measure of our belief in an afterlife may be our desire not to deny future generations an earthly starting point for their pilgrimage. Survival has become a new spiritual imperative.

In traditional spirituality, survival was always considered a rather primitive state of being. Mere survival conjures up subhuman images: in the natural order it implies eating, sleeping, and procreating. Similarly, in the social order it connotes making a living, looking out for number one, security at all costs. In any case, survival is seen as a low-level form of life which sacrifices nothing for such higher values as love and justice.

Yet in a nuclear age, survival may become primary rather than primitive. When we begin to face the possibility of humanly imposed mass death, then life becomes the primary (although not the only) value. In the extreme situation of the contemporary world, the survivors of Auschwitz have become examples of how endurance is the final form of freedom.

Today we are called to care for the earth and for the human race in a more than human way. Such care is not a primitive act. It is a pious response. Unlike the animals, we must consciously choose to care for our own species. But, unlike the survival tacticians, we can no longer choose to salvage our own existence at the expense of that of others. In a negative way, the possibility of nuclear destruction is forcing us to understand what our scriptures told us long ago: we are all members of the same race. We are all inhabitants of the same earth. We either survive together, or not at all.

It is difficult for us to choose, to consciously become what we already are — members of the human race. How much more obvious is the choice to become a member of a religion or of a nation. Nevertheless, the precedent has been unequivocally set. The person who most consciously chose to become a member of the human race was God in the person of Jesus Christ.

God saw that the earth was a good place to begin. God granted the earth and His son as guarantees of a new creation. But the guarantees are mutual guarantees and God does not take our responsibility for granted.

In this dark night we must contemplate the possible: the destruction of God's creation, the image of God in the human person defaced beyond recognition, the ashes of Christ's body, in his brothers and sisters today, strewn across the wasteland. Desecration.

The nuclear tomb does not force us to believe in a future resurrection, it calls us to face our present blasphemy.

What grounds do we have to hope that God will make a new beginning? To hope in the resurrection will mean beginning to hope in ourselves as much as God hopes in us. It will mean believing in the power of Christ to resurrect us from our present personal and political paralysis. It will mean loving life limitlessly.

The community of survivors may be not unlike the community of saints.

## NOW THE HOUR HAS COME
### (TS, April 3, 1982)

Word has it that the cruise missile will be tested in Alberta this summer. More than a missile is being tested. We are all being tested—as religious people, as human beings.

There are certain historical moments when the metal of Christianity is tested for its purity, when the fire of the times becomes so intense that only the most unalloyed beliefs endure.

Such a moment came fifty years ago in Europe. As Hitler stoked the furnaces of fanaticism, the gospel metal of the churches was tested.

Most people took out fire insurance for their churches, schools, and homes. Public and private concordats were signed with the state.

As many watched the inferno from a distance, their integrity went up in smoke. Some felt the heat. A few resisted and got burned—their golden lives the only remnant of the costly commandment to love.

For many years, Christians in Central and South

America have been feeling the heat. The extremes of wealth and poverty, of domination and oppression, have fueled a crucible of faith. In such situations, neutrality is the delusion of an icy heart or the insulation of a fearful one. When the lives of the poor are being reduced to ashes, one is either fanning the flames or pulling people out of the furnace. There is no other option. Even bystanders fan the flames with the blink of their eyes.

We have yet to see how the church in those countries will emerge from this human crucible. But we must see that the time of testing has now come for Christians in North America.

Since Hiroshima and Nagasaki we have been helping to prepare for the incineration of the human race. Now the explosive hour has come. As in Germany, as in Central America, we are faced with a choice: either we build the earth into a nuclear furnace or we tear down the furnace to make room for human habitation.

There is no other option. Shooting the breeze about nuclear deterrence just adds to the hot air.

Some will argue that we as Canadians have no option at all. They will say that the choice is up to the superpowers — not to the likes of us. Fireproofing. The insulation of innocence.

However, the cruise missile exposes our sense of helpless innocence as an illusion of our branch-plant morality. How accustomed we are to lay the blame at the door of the head office, which is elsewhere. It is true that the cruise missile was conceived in the United States — but it is being hatched in our back yard.

Litton Industries in Rexdale is the technological nest where the navigational brain systems of the missiles are being constructed. There are many nuclear eggs being hatched at Litton, each with a destructive capacity fifteen times that of the bomb dropped on Hiroshima.

The cruise missiles will come to maturity in the United States, but they will take their first flights in Alberta. Not unexpectedly. Our cruising chickens are coming home to roost.


## THE CHURCH IN FERMENT
### (CNT, April 18, 1982)

A feature article in the *Globe and Mail* (March 20) carries the descriptive headline "The Church in Turmoil". A subsequent column by Larry Henderson in the *Catholic Register* (April 3) asks, "Is the Church in Turmoil?" and answers, no — only in the minds of dissident Catholics and disaffected intellectuals. The superficiality of the former article is matched only by the sincerity of the latter.

Let us recall another time of turmoil in the church, a time when theologians were locked in near mortal combat over the revolutionary ideas of a pagan thinker. Many theologians and clerics defended the faith, or what they had defined as the faith. They dismissed the ideas of the pagan, or what they thought were his ideas. They found comfort in their composed theologies and the piety of the faithful.

A few theologians greeted the insights of the pagan thinker with reckless enthusiasm. Their openness was, more often than not, indicative of intellectual shallowness and a fragile faith.

One theologian, however, took the pagan thinker and his disturbing ideas seriously. He pondered. To the shock of his conservative contemporaries, he began to write about the positive contributions of the pagan. To the amazement of his more liberal contemporaries, he began to improve and hone the pagan insights within a new theological framework.

His daring and dynamic theological venture was greeted with derision by most of his colleagues. The bishop publicly condemned most of his positions. After his death, the leaders of his religious community constantly had to reassure the members that their brother theologian was "acceptable".

The time? The thirteenth century. The theologian? Saint Thomas Aquinas, now Doctor of the Church. The pagan thinker? Aristotle.

Many Catholics today think fondly of Thomas Aquinas as the paradigm of traditional theology, and of his times as the blessed age of the church ordered in tranquillity. Such misconceptions can arise if one has only read Saint Thomas as he was domesticated in the scholastic manuals of the nineteenth century or in the Baltimore catechism of this century. What is often referred to as the tradition of the church is really only a very limited period within that tradition – the last hundred years.

Fortunately, eminent Catholic thinkers such as Jacques Maritain, Etienne Gilson, Karl Rahner, and Bernard Lonergan have recovered the essentially Catholic approach of Saint Thomas.

In his openness to the turmoil of his times, Saint Thomas exemplified the finest attitude of the Catholic tradition. The depth of his faith is evident in the extent to which he was able to seek and find God in all dimensions of life. He believed that any authentic human question would lead one to God. He did not defend the church from the questions of his time. He took those questions seriously and, hearing them out, directed them to their ultimate end. He was willing to rethink any category which confined God and our approach to Him.

We too live in a time when our faith can seem fragile in the face of rampant secularism. We can dismiss the disturbing questions posed by "pagan" thinkers such as

Freud and Marx. We can dismiss those who attempt to take such disturbing thoughts seriously as "dissidents" or "disaffected intellectuals". Yet to do so is to betray our own Catholic tradition.

The well-defended church may ward off the evil influences of our day but it will also ward off the good influences. It will also find itself unable to open its doors to those who are earnestly seeking the Way, the Truth, and the Life.

To the extent that we are a believing church, we will be able to step into the turmoil of our times with the conviction that this is the ferment where the seeds of the gospel will flourish anew.

In the thirteenth century, most Catholics were quite content with the vision of faith as it was presented to them in the time-honoured neo-Platonic categories. They saw no need for the new framework of faith being constructed by Thomas Aquinas. Yet it is probable that without this "dissident" theologian, the church would not have been able to bring its long tradition forward into the modern age.

Our task today is not completely unlike that of Saint Thomas. As Catholics faithful to our tradition, we are invited to take seriously the disturbing questions posed by technology, by women, by the non-Western world, etc. If we hear these questions out, we may find that they will lead us to God rather than away from Him. If our church responds to the turmoil of these times (not uncritically but constructively) we may be building a bridge which will carry our tradition over into the next century.

Is the church in turmoil? Perhaps. But — perhaps more important — it is in ferment.

*April 24, 1982*
It all began with a phone call at the office from what sounded like a little old lady with a frail voice. "We want

you to come to Vancouver and speak at our peace rally," she said. I told her that I was sure there were lots of people in Vancouver who could fill the bill. "We need someone from elsewhere," she replied. "You see, we're having trouble convincing the bishop here that peace is important. He's made it seem un-Catholic to participate in peace rallies. The priests can't really say much. So we thought it would be nice to have a token Catholic nun from elsewhere to put a kind of blessing on it." I laughed at the chutzpah of it all, and went.

Meeting Mildred Fahrni and her friend Daisy Webster was an inspiring experience. These two old women have been active in peace work since the forties in the States. They've just kept plugging along, and in fact they organized this massive peace rally. They make sure that the heads of all the organizations take the more visible roles so they feel committed to getting their membership out. There is such a lack of ego in these women, real purity of heart. It's good to meet these long-haul types.

### HIS NAME IS CHRISTOPHER
(CNT, May 16, 1982)

He is very small and he lives in an incubator. Born only three weeks ago, he will probably not live beyond the end of May. A rare genetic syndrome.

This is a hard fact for his parents, who have waited so expectantly. This is a hard fact for those of us who have treasured the hope of his parents, a hope conceived after several miscarriages. This child was not only their act of love; he was also their act of faith. They named him Christopher—the Christ bearer.

The news of his birth was quickly overshadowed by the medical verdict that he would not be with us for long. I went to the hospital with little to say. It is rather easy to speak about the state of the world but not so easy to talk about a child who is the whole world to his parents.

Yet, over these past few weeks, it is Christopher who has said a great deal to each of us. As we sit and watch his small smiles and reach through the incubator to hold his hands, he is teaching us about the mystery of creation — about the mystery of our own creation.

We are amazed at the miracle that is Christopher. With him, a whole new world has begun.

When I see Christopher, I feel that the reality of my eventual death is somehow encompassed by the miracle of my own beginning.

How easily we take our lives for granted. How often we dwell on the in-between time of our lives, on the hills and valleys of our adult years. It takes a Christopher to remind us that there is all the difference in the world between being born and not being at all.

How happy we would be if we never got over the miracle of having been born.

Christopher is a whole new world for his parents and for those of us who love the three of them. He has introduced a tenderness and tears, a fragility and faith, that we had not known before. He is the beginning of something new in each one of us.

Being with Christopher, our faith is slowly reborn again. "He is our angel," says his father, "who will go before us to prepare the way."

There will be hard times ahead for his parents. That we know. Yet I believe there will also be times when a hand will reach out to help them, when a tender look will grace their day, when they will feel a childlike joy bubble up from within, when they will look about them and say, "It is very good."

And they will know he is near.

There is no moral to this story—only a mystery. His name is Christopher.

*July 1982*

We have finally issued our major article outlining the cutbacks to CCODP. The facts are there for anyone who wants to read them. Have received a lot of calls from the media about the story, and from many people who are congratulating us. I tell them the most helpful thing they can do is to write a letter to *Catholic New Times* to show their concern. I have been shocked how few people are willing to show their support publicly. It's all "off the record". They are very happy we have gone out on a limb but they don't want to get out there with us—especially if their jobs are on the line. These are people who say they are concerned about social justice. And they talk a lot about being prophetic. Many of them are working in and for CCODP; they have everything to gain from this exposé and we have everything to lose. I must say I am a little disillusioned with the fair-weather people on the left. It's easy to be for justice if it doesn't cost you anything. You can never be really free and truthful as long as you are afraid of losing your job.

One of the most interesting phone calls I received was from a bishop working in the Vatican. He said he had a conscience and was disturbed at the pattern of secrecy around church finances. He had lots of stories to tell but no real evidence on paper. "Nothing important in Rome gets put down on paper," he said.

Out of curiosity, I asked him who was the most powerful church leader in Canada. (I wanted to find out whether there was anyone who would challenge Cardinal Carter on the cutback of funds.) I almost swallowed the phone when he answered, "Stephen Roman" (the head of Denison Mines). "He invites some Vatican cardinals to his place in the Caribbean every year and gives them money and gifts and then tells them who he thinks should be appointed as Canadian bishops." Considering the source, it's hard to know what to think. Either it's true and then God help us, or it's false — another bishop trying to manipulate the press for his own purposes.

## EVIL RARELY WEARS A HUMAN FACE
### (TS, June 26, 1982)

The tenth anniversary of Watergate has been duly noted in the media.

What could have been the occasion for sober reflection has become, instead, an opportunity for interesting updates on all those characters who played their parts in the drama that climaxed with the exit of the President of the United States.

We have been informed that many of these characters are prolonging (and thus profiting from) the drama of Watergate.

Yet there is a much deeper sense in which this drama is not over. It is being played out in many theatres of our society. It is a drama of evil — but one quite different from the medieval allegories in which evil wore an ugly mask.

I remember watching the Watergate proceedings on TV — waiting for the villain to appear. He never did. There was only a parade of fools and functionaries, petty thieves and con men. Nixon himself was the ultimate in mediocrity.

Way deep down, he was really very superficial.

To characterize these men as villains is to overestimate them. They were ordinary people — some of them rather nice. They had families and friends. They got on with the job. It is hard for them to recall that they did anything really bad. This is how the drama of evil is frequently played out in our society. Evil is enacted not by villains but by ordinary people.

It is easy to miss the importance of this scenario. The religious traditions of our culture have accustomed us to thinking of evil in terms of people. We assume that bad deeds are done by bad people, that evil is wrought by the wicked. We expect evil to have a face and a name.

This assumption is carried over by many socially conscious people. If bad things are happening in our country, they say, then it is the fault of bankers and politicians — who must be bad people. What must then be explained away are the disturbingly good personal qualities that bankers and politicians sometimes display.

However, the moral dilemma of our times is that evil only rarely wears a human face. Search for the causes of many of the evils in our society and you will find — not a villain — but a faceless, nameless system that no one seems to control. This is the systematic form of evil, which organizational bureaucracies and technology have introduced into the contemporary world.

The evil of a system is difficult to get hold of. You can't touch and feel a system. The core of such systematic evil is perhaps best described by Augustine's ancient phrase, "Evil is a nothingness."

Nevertheless, while the systematic cause of evil disappears into unreality, the effect on people's lives is very real: people go hungry, they are unemployed, they are driven to drink.

One of the most deadening characteristics of any system is that it insulates those within it from the consequences of their own actions. It creates conditions through which nice and ordinary people contribute to evil results without even realizing it.

With nodding heads, the committee members bow to

economic necessity. With fingertip control the secretary types out the memo. With a stroke of a pen, the executive eliminates funding for hundreds of people. With a flick of the wrist the clerk files away the cries for reconsideration. Not one of them feels responsible for this wreckage of human lives. They don't have to face the desperate eyes of those who bear the burdens of the decision.

Hence Watergate. Hence the evil that continues to be done — not by the wicked but by the thoughtless.

None of us is blameless in this regard for we all participate in one system or another: economic, social, political, educational, even religious. The greatest illusion is to think we can do no evil simply because we are ordinary or well intentioned.

*July 1982*
I keep thinking about Mother Teresa. She and I had a chance to talk as we were waiting to speak to the large peace rally sponsored by Youth Corps in Toronto. There were so many things I thought I "ought" to say to her: couldn't you say more about the causes of poverty? Couldn't you say more about injustice in the church? Don't you know people are using you to put down nuns in North America?

But the questions seemed all wrong. She may not say all the politically correct things about peace, but she is at peace. Everything about her is worn — her hands are rough, the soles of her feet are cracked, her shoes are battered, her face is lined with care. She is worn out from loving. And she is radiant. Mercy, mercy everywhere. In the end I didn't want to talk with her, just wanted to be with her.

*August 1982*
I have been profoundly shaken by the revelations in Irving Abella and Harold Troper's new book, *None Is Too Many*.

It seems our wonderfully tolerant country had the worst record in the Western world in terms of letting in Jewish refugees in the thirties and forties. "To the condemned Jews of Auschwitz, Canada had a special meaning. It was the name given to the camp barracks where the food, clothes, gold, diamonds, jewellery and other goods taken from prisoners were stored. It represented life, luxury and salvation; it was a Garden of Eden in Hell; it was also unreachable.

"In effect, the barracks at Auschwitz symbolized what Canada was to all the Jews of Europe throughout the 1930s and 1940s – a paradise, enormous, wealthy, overflowing and full of life; but out of bounds, a haven totally inaccessible."

And now we continue to shut out the refugees.

*September 1982*
When I learned that Sharelife had raised $700,000 more than expected from the 1980-81 campaign, I phoned Paul Robinson to ask where that money would be going. Why couldn't it go to Development and Peace, I asked, since funds for that organization had been cut by $750,000?

He was flustered and invited me out for lunch. I met him at the Quo Vadis restaurant – a place where he seemed well known to all the waiters. In the course of an extravagant meal (paid for with a Sharelife credit card), Robinson urged me to stop writing about the Development and Peace money. He assured me that he was already doing everything he could to change policies from the inside. I promised him only that I would try to write the truth fairly.

After the luncheon I reflected on how easily Robinson seemed to believe that enough fine food and flattery could make one forgetful of the hungry of this world. And I wondered how and when and where he had come to believe this. I wondered whether this sad and foolish man was a cause or a symptom of some of the inconsistencies in the Sharelife organization.

Since we've moved to Parkdale from the trendy Annex I'm finding myself more uncomfortable in a place like Quo Vadis. The issue of poverty has many more names and faces. The ex-mental patients shuffle along the street. Vacant. So many with nothing to do, no place to go. Leftovers. Poverty is a dispiriting reality here.

TIME TO QUESTION SHARELIFE

(TS, Oct. 2, 1982)

I greet the news of the beginning of this year's Sharelife appeal with profoundly mixed feelings.

On the one hand, this annual appeal by the Roman Catholic Archdiocese of Toronto is a marvellous example of grassroots generosity and participation. Sharelife has been a yearly revelation of the reservoir of decency and compassion which can be drawn upon in this city.

On the other hand, it is disturbing to see how the money flowing from this reservoir is being channelled. While the level of funding has risen dramatically over the past three years, the once steady stream of support for the people of the third world has been proportionately slowing to a trickle. This flow of funds has been increasingly diverted to the streets of Toronto.

When the Sharelife appeal began six years ago, almost half the money raised went to the third world—and it went through a church agency which addressed the causes, rather than the symptoms, of poverty. Last year this agency—the Canadian Catholic Organization for Development and Peace (CCODP)—received approximately one-tenth of the money raised through Sharelife. Yet the rechannelling of funds has happened so subtly that many Catholics still think half the money they give to Sharelife will go to development projects in the third world.

The change became more obvious in June of last year, when it was announced that the anticipated funds for CCODP World ($1.25 million) would be cut by $750,000 to establish a new pastoral mission program. Because of matching government funds, that cut meant a loss of $1.5 to $3 million for third-world development projects. No one asked the people involved in those projects whether they could do with less.

In itself, the new Toronto program emphasizing evangelization in the third world is a good thing. However, it is difficult to understand why this program was created at the expense of CCODP work. It is even more difficult to understand why the money for the new pastoral projects was not raised through one of a number of collections established in the church for just such purposes.

Last year's Sharelife collection went (at least) $700,000 over the top. Where will this extra money go? A few initial inquiries indicate that almost all will be ploughed back into local Toronto charities.

This money should go to the work of CCODP in the third world. Until this unfinished business is settled, it is difficult to celebrate the beginning of another Sharelife appeal.

It is unfortunate that the Archdiocese of Toronto (like so many other institutions) has cut back on its commitment to justice in the third world when that commitment is sorely needed. I cannot accept this lack of fidelity — but I can partly understand it. In hard economic times, the old maxim that "charity begins at home" seems more relevant. The decision-makers at Sharelife seem to believe this: last year they gave twice as much money to the Under 21 program for street kids as to the whole of the third world.

Such an attitude can be an unfortunate variation of an

older form of parochialism, a parochialism that has never reflected the best tradition of a church that claims to be universal.

I can understand how the needs of kids on the streets of our city can seem so much more urgent and compelling than those of unknown and unseen millions.

Yet Sharelife itself began six years ago because of an unpopular but highly moral commitment to the unborn, who were not being treated with equal concern by the United Way. For someone living in Toronto, the unborn and the poor of the third world are alike in some very basic ways: they are unseen, they are unheard, they are unknown. Yet they have rights and they exert a moral claim on our world every bit as much as those who have arrived on our small scene.

It is my deep conviction that Sharelife must listen to the cry for justice in the third world. To respond to that cry with a strong financial commitment would help reclaim the soul of Sharelife.

*October 15, 1982*
Last night a bomb was planted and exploded at Litton Industries. Seven people were injured. It is a tragedy for them but also a tragedy for the peace movement. We are all being tarred with the same brush — we are dangerous, we are violent, we are risks to national security. Several people have had their offices and homes raided. We have cleared out anything that we don't want taken away from *Catholic New Times* — like all the research on Sharelife. We know we face an uphill battle to regain any credibility for the peace movement in this city.

*November 1982*
Janet Somerville (my cohort at CNT) and I had an interesting discussion about our basic stances that I want to set

down and reflect on. She has found this whole confrontation over Sharelife difficult because she tends naturally to be more tolerant and more anxious to be in some kind of unity with the representatives of the official church.

*MJ*: You're always trying to see both sides of an issue—or all sides. It makes it difficult to write an editorial, to take a position. By the time we qualify everything, we qualify ourselves out of a position. We're neutralized. I'm suspicious of neutrality. It feels amoral, self-protective.   .

*Janet*: The really difficult thing about Christianity is loving other Christians. Are you willing to let them be the Body of Christ?

*MJ*: I think you're confusing personal relationships with public stances. I agree about how we should be with one another personally, but that shouldn't be projected as a model for taking social and political positions. We can't love another position.

*Janet*: I'm arguing for a respectful welcome for another position.

*MJ*: I agree, but it seems to me in the end that not all positions are compatible. You can't say yes to everything.

*Janet*: I don't want that either. But I don't want to write as if our position was *the* expression of the gospel.

*MJ*: But there are some issues on which we have to say clearly that this *is* the gospel imperative—like capital punishment, El Salvador....

*Janet*: You can be prayerful and just, and still believe that capital punishment should be a legal possibility.

*MJ*: I think you're saying the gospel admits of many

positions. I'm saying there are times when we must say—this is *not* a gospel position.

*Janet*: Those times are rare.

MJ: And they may be more often than we are willing to admit. You have a gift for pursuing the effort to reconcile or at least understand a different position.

*Janet*: You have a gift for identifying the need to choose.

MJ: But your gift relies on someone else having taken a position! I'm not sure what's the more costly way. If you take a position there's always the possibility of being wrong, of failing, of a breaking of relationships.

*Janet*: If you work at reconciling you can get pulled every which way. It does affect relationships. They don't get broken but they get twisted under the weight of what's going on. No one quite trusts you— at least, not as an ally, not as a comrade. But you know, I don't work at seeing the good in other positions only in order to preserve relationships. I do it also for the sake of the breadth and subtlety of truth. Reality is very complicated; with my temperament, I do see an endless shading of for and against.

MJ: I probably see as many shades. But for me, the Christian option is to give yourself totally in a real, imperfect situation, taking a real, imperfect position, knowing it has its limits. If you don't give yourself totally in the historic moment, then there isn't a real incarnation. Words have to become flesh.

*Janet*: I find that moving. When you say it that way, it lets me see that maybe that's why I hold back on positions.... Maybe I'm just refusing to give myself totally, in the historic moment. I agree that you don't have Incarnation without that kind of generosity, that kind of risk and solidarity.

Isn't there another dimension when it's a question

of disagreements within the church? You can't belong to the church as the Body of Christ without the dimension of surrender, somehow. Letting the bishops be leaders and teachers in the Lord only happens if we co-constitute their office by our concrete respect for their ministry of holding the church together. The church isn't God, but it's the body of Christ in history, made up 100 per cent of sinners. That's more important than a position.

*MJ*: What I agree with is that we only surrender to persons. But for me that is not automatically a bishop. It's people, people in the church, the person of Jesus.

*Janet*: We both have to accept to love what is broken and afflicted — and to love passionately.

*December 19, 1982*
Janet phoned me with the news that Paul Robinson had been arrested for stealing money from Sharelife. Now it all comes clear. That's why he was so anxious to stop us from asking questions about where the money was going. It seems he bottlenecked the Sharelife money that was supposed to be sent on to the head office of Development and Peace and pocketed the interest from the fund. For us, at least, this story may be over. The sleaze of it all. Robinson another of those mushrooms that flourishes in the dark secrecy of the church.

THE CHILD OF OUR FAITH AND LOVE
(CNT, Dec. 26, 1982)

This is the season when we are brought home to ourselves by the child who has made all the difference in the world. The Christ-child.

In this child we are offered, as Mary was, a God who

has made himself weak and vulnerable. He gives Himself over to our hands, to our hearts.

We, like Mary and Joseph, are not compelled to care for this child. We can ignore this child, as we are free to ignore the child within ourselves and in others. We can shut our ears to his cry, as we can deny the cry of many children who hunger for food and so much more. We can refuse to let our lives be interrupted by this child, as we can to let events break into our patterned world. We are free to accept or neglect the burden of our faith and love.

In many times and in many ways, God comes to us in this childlike vulnerability. He is given over to us in each other, and we are free to be caring or careless of his needs. He is given over to us in a fragile world, and we are free to nurture or to neglect that struggling world. He is given over to our hands in the Eucharist, and we are free to cherish His gesture of trust or to cast it aside.

He is given over to us in the church, as we are free to walk with Him through the night of these times or to sleep on in ourselves. He is the child who lives among us, who draws us together and calls us to become adults in faith.

How often, during the year, we find it difficult to bear with this child who is with us always. We run out of time, out of patience, out of love. How can we bear with the multi-faceted child of our faith when we have barely come of age?

At the limits of our endurance, we experience the profound paradox of our lives as Christians: we can become adult and responsible — we can let others hold our hand when they are afraid of the dark, hungry for love, or thirsty for justice — because we ourselves can, sometimes, become as little children and reach out to hold the hand of our Father and Mother who are in heaven.

*New Year's Day, 1983*

Luigi was with us last night! Effervescent as ever, he rolled in wearing a baseball cap. It's his sign of protest against the Latin American chic of the left. He held forth at some length about the conservative clampdown in the Peruvian church and about the increasing fanaticism of the leftist guerrillas (the Shining Path). What's amazing is that he had us all chuckling along with him. Most Latin American advocates rely heavily on guilt to get a little action. Luigi has little time for North American types who legitimize their own anger in the name of justice. "The problem with them is that they're too sad. They don't look like they really enjoy life. We don't trust them if they don't like to sing and dance. A political movement that can't celebrate doesn't have any future."

Isabel turned up the music. We took what he said to heart because we know his life is deadly serious at times.

Luigi took me aside and told me he thought we tended to romanticize the Latin American poor in CNT. "Some of the articles make them out to be noble savages. Sometimes the poor aren't so noble. So what? Jesus never came for the noble savages." He suggested we spend more time writing about the oppression of the middle class here. "I need to say to those in captivity 'Go free.' You need to say to those who think they are free, 'You are in captivity.' "

I told him how disappointed I had been with the left during the Sharelife crisis. Even more disappointed than I was with church officials. "Sometimes I feel I'm fighting against lies for the sake of a half-truth." It happens, he said. "If you follow Jesus you find yourself thrown together with a lot of people you'd rather not associate with. So big deal."

Luigi's experience in Peru seems to have given him a clarity about what's a "big deal" and what isn't. He told Mark that he didn't even find celibacy a problem any more. "Once I started working with the people, celibacy made all kinds of sense." Mark said he almost envied such clarity. "My challenge is how to speak about God to people who believe Coke is the real thing." Luigi's response: "My people believe God is real. But my challenge, buddy, is how to say God is love to people who have been so abused."

The conversations with Luigi have thrown me back on the question Northrop Frye thinks we Canadians should ask: "Where is Here?"

Last night it was Luigi who seemed most able to reach out to Bill and Susan. They astounded us with the announcement that they are going to try to have another child.

Towards the end of the evening, the conversation turned to the Israeli invasion of Lebanon. I was expecting this and dreading it. Ann is disturbed by the right-wing tendencies in the Israeli government. Who isn't? But on the question of Israel I do feel caught in the middle. An uncomfortable place for me to be. Are there times and places when the middle ground is the only moral place to be?

I told the group I had been invited to go to Lebanon — one of many invitations. Confessed how often I feel overwhelmed by the demands for some public presence, talks etc. I know that sometimes (often?) I've been used in situations. Mark thought that was outrageous. But I think there's a difference between being used and choosing to be used — letting yourself, your name, what you stand for, be used for a purpose.

Less ambiguous is the beginning of a little peace group — Christian Initiative for Peace — formed to try to pick up some of the pieces after the Litton bombing. Len Desroches, a veteran activist, came and asked me to join in getting the group started. We know only a group of prayerful, committed people are going to be able to weather the storm of suspicion unleashed by the bombing.

LET PHARAOH GO
(TS, Feb. 19, 1983)

There is one North American myth about women's liberation that must be dispelled. Liberation does not happen overnight. It is a long and slow process.

I say this, not because I am less committed to women's liberation, but because I am more conscious of the depth of domination that exists within a chauvinistic culture and an even more chauvinistic church.

For all the sophistication of many feminist groups, they seem strangely naive about the process of real liberation. Their frustration with the slowness of change is as naive as it is legitimate.

It is instructive to listen to the critics of women's liberation. While their motives are open to dispute, some of their observations cannot be denied. Liberated women are domineering and overpowering, they say. Liberated women are oppressive, they conclude. Such comments could easily be dismissed as a refusal to face the future were it not for one sad fact from history — more often than not, the oppressed who have won their struggle become the new oppressors.

Why is that the case? I return to the scriptures to reflect on the Exodus, the event in the Judeo-Christian tradition that serves as a model of liberation.

There is a short version of this powerful story of the passage from slavery to freedom: the Jewish people were oppressed by Pharaoh; they spent forty years in the desert; they made a covenant with God on Sinai; and then they entered the Promised Land. This would seem to support the North American myth that liberation, if not painless, is at least a rather quick process.

But scholars of scripture now relate a much longer version of the Exodus story. Their research indicates that the stay in the desert was much longer than the metaphorical forty years would suggest. Moses and his people may have wandered for generations, for as long as four hundred years.

This new information is sufficient to give one pause. It pushes me to reconsider the significance of the desert time in the process of liberation.

The desert was the time in between the experience of bondage and the exercise of political and religious freedom. The desert was the period in which the people could begin to shed the self-image of slaves, the image that had been imposed upon them by the power of Pharaoh.

It took a long time for the people to forget the politics of the brickyard they had learned in Egypt—a politics based on relationships of dominance and dependence. And the Hebrew scriptures tell us how difficult it was not to carry forth the patterns of Pharaoh into the desert. The people wanted control and security. They built idols.

Such behaviour is more an indictment of Pharaoh's domination than an indication of the people's capacity for freedom. Pharaoh's pattern of domination had become so internalized that it threatened to shape not only their past but their future as well. So it is with women or with any oppressed group that has long been dominated. When power becomes possible, it is usually exercised in the only way it has been experienced—oppressively. Pharaoh may yet wear a feminine face.

Such reflections should only deepen our condemnation of the exercise of Pharaoh-like power in the pyramidal structures of church and society. Yet such reflections should also serve to caution those women who think the

Promised Land is just over the horizon. When the haul gets longer, the temptation to idolize power positions and the priesthood becomes stronger.

To leave the way of Pharaoh and find the way of freedom, men and women must go consciously into the desert. There we must shed the images of self that have been graven within. There we must forget the politics of the brickyard. There we must live unknowing and with uncertainty. Then we may be ready for covenants and what is promised.

I do not know what the contemporary equivalent of four hundred years of sand is. I do not know where that desert is for us today, personally, practically, politically. I do believe that desert time and space are necessary.

### THE GOSPEL OF AISHIYE
#### (CNT, March 13, 1983)

The cross was there — hanging over the altar on a bullet-ridden wall. One of the legs of the plaster Jesus had been shot away, just as sixty people had been shot away in the small church of the village of Aishiye. I stood there, unable to kneel, unable to stand, beneath the only cross that revealed the suffering of Lebanon today.

The serenity of the church was shattered by the assaulting knowledge that, six years before, guerrillas had herded terrified villagers into the sanctuary and.... Now only the silence screams. One arm of Jesus dangles from a nail.

It was a long journey to this place of crucifixion. I had been travelling throughout Israel, listening to the many voices engaged in the intense debate that followed upon the Israeli invasion of Lebanon in June 1982. During each interview, my mind was stretched by new facets and facts. As I talked with Palestinians and Israelis, I saw their shared history as a tragic conflict between two rights over-shadowed by a whole history of wrongs. But my heart had yet to be stretched. That stretching began to happen as I crossed from Israel into southern Lebanon. At the border town of Metulla, in one of those seedy hotels which always flourish on the edge of a war zone, I met a group of French journalists. I went with them behind a military convoy through the various checkpoints.

That was three months ago. I should have reported on that journey almost immediately. After all, I had inter-viewed some of the highest officials in the Begin govern-ment, the spokesperson for the Peace Now movement, the editor of the *Jerusalem Post*, and a Palestinian mayor on the West Bank.

I could not write. Weeks passed and a hot story grew cold between the sheets of my notebook.

But now it is Lent. It is not a better time to write, but it is the right time to bear witness. Lent is the season of the broken-hearted and that is the only heart with which I could embrace the whole of the broken reality of Lebanon.

Much has been written about the recent war in Leba-non, perhaps too much. In lectures, colloquia, and inter-views, much has been said. Yet how much has been felt?

As I journeyed through the war-torn area of southern Lebanon, I began to despise rapid-fire journalists with their quick shots of life and death. I knew I would find myself forever uneasy in concerned North American dis-cussions about the "issues" of the Middle East. Inevitably the question would be asked—"Whose side are you on?" I knew I would not find an answer, for it lay buried some-where in the ruined villages of southern Lebanon.

The roads in that area took our car through stark hills which seemed to stand as the only victors from years of armed struggle.

Only from a distance did the hillside villages seem

bathed in the invincible Mediterranean sunlight. At the end of every sideroad we came upon the discreet but devastating signs of war.

A few people watched us as if they had seen it all before. I had not seen it all before. I had not seen homes reduced to a twisted mass of stone and metal. Concrete convulsions.

I walked slowly around one heap of rubble and blinked. Here a mother had cooked breakfast, a child had cried in its sleep, the men had talked about the weather. What relics of daily life lay buried in that tomb? Who had dealt these concrete blows to the humble process of living? Some say it was the Israelis; others say it was the Palestinians, or the Syrians, or the Lebanese Christians.

Yet if you walk through the skeletal stone reality of the villages of southern Lebanon, you sense that it would take a very long time to conclude who did what to whom. Some of the collapsed homes are encased in rust and covered with vegetation — remnants of an onslaught six years ago. There are other homes which bear more recent scars — the white flash of freshly broken stone.

Over the years since the outbreak of civil war, these small villages have been attacked by different groups for various reasons. But always the result is the same. Only the stones cry out.

Who can hear such a cry? If once it pierces the heart, the solidity of issues collapses and the stone-walling of taking sides begins to crumble.

With a broken heart, you can walk through the villages of southern Lebanon carrying all the pieces of that fractured reality. You carry the memory of Nazi Europe, which finally drove the Jews to claim the promised place of security. You carry the desperation of the Palestinians, who have been condemned to a wandering indignity. You carry the lament of the Lebanese for their once lovely land. That is the way of the cross in Lebanon today. It led me finally to the village of Aishiye.

The most visible signs of life were the huge posters of Bashir and Amin Gemayel which were plastered on every space of wall. Here and there people were picking up the remnants of their lives. Some old people wandered onto the road, two small children played in what must once have been a yard.

We talked with some of the people with the aid of a translator. The story came out in slow spurts of sorrow. In 1976, this was a peaceful village. There were about three thousand of us Christians. One day the Palestinian guerrillas came. They destroyed our homes. They took some of our people into the church and shot them. There were children too. That is why the cross is broken. Everyone left except the oldest.

In terms of body-count politics, this was not a large massacre. Your heart feels the enormity of it only when an old man shows you the picture of his five sons and one grandson. "My children...all killed." These children were the whole world to him.

Yet I could not let myself cry with him. I was suspicious. One of the casualties of the recent war in Lebanon is the truth. Stories of massacres have become standard propaganda for all sides involved in the conflict. In the wake of the horrible massacres of the refugees in Shatila and Sabra, both the Lebanese and the Israelis have been all too ready to point out that the Palestinians have dipped their hands in blood.

Wondering how to confirm or deny my suspicions, I asked if there was a priest in the village. Yes — he had just returned.

We found him in a makeshift dwelling farther up the road, and to our relief we found that we would not have to rely on a translator. Somewhat reluctantly, he told us that he had been the one who had buried his murdered parishioners in a common grave. Then he had gone to live with his daughter in Canada until it was safe to return.

He was a Maronite priest and we expected him to lend a sympathetic voice to the political struggles of the Lebanese Christians. The journalist from Paris fed him a leading question: "Well, Father, what do you think of the Palestinians after what they did to you people?" All pens in the room were poised to write.

"I forgive all — especially our enemies," replied the priest.

That was not the answer the French journalist wanted to hear, nor the one for which I was prepared. The question was restated: "But how can you say that after what the Palestinians have done to your people?"

The priest looked at him sadly and said, "God's ways are not our ways. In this village I will not preach revenge. Our Lord Jesus Christ commands us to forgive our enemies."

The French journalist left without a story. I left with a message of hope. It is the gospel according to Aishiye.

Before my arrival in Aishiye, I had listened to many groups cite the long history of the wrongs that had been committed against them. That history was used to justify further wrongdoing in the present. I had been travelling in a circle of bad to worse.

The priest's words broke through that vicious and tragic circle. With his words of forgiveness, there was the possibility of breaking with the patterns of the past which threatened to overwhelm the present. His forgiveness meant, not forgetting the past, but believing in the possibility of a new beginning. Aishiye was the place where, for one brief moment, peace seemed like a possibility for the poor of this earth.

Such a gospel of forgiveness cannot be easily translated

into political and social decisions. Yet the fact that one man even uttered those revolutionary words is hopeful enough to go on.

Forgiveness is not a gospel which we can preach from a distance. A heart must be pierced by the suffering of Lebanon before it can speak a redeeming word. The priest who bore within himself the broken reality of his world could speak the words which sound as gracious today as they did two thousand years ago.

From his cross in Aishiye, Jesus is forgiving those who have broken his body in his brothers and sisters. Let the broken-hearted draw near and stand at the foot of his cross.

## Lent 1983

So our little peace group, Christian Initiative for Peace, has been meeting once a week in the very early morning. Quite by chance we have hit upon a way of ensuring real commitment on the part of the members: the only real requirement for membership in CIP is that people come to the weekly meeting at six in the morning. That way you know you will be able to count on them. This helps deal with the "flake factor" that is so prevalent in the peace movement.

There is tremendous energy and resolve in the group — out of all proportion to its size. And it is quite a cross-section of people — all ages and shapes and stripes. The one thing we have in common is the commitment — which is everything.

### LET PEACE DAWN*

As Easter rises in our hearts,

* Easter Sunday 1983 Statement from the Christian Initiative for Peace (written with members of CIP)

we respond to an urgent call
to move beyond the darkness of these times
by committing ourselves to peace.
For many weeks, we have gathered
in the early hours of each Thursday morning
to pray and plan for peace.
Between the last hour of darkness
and the first hour of dawn,
we have faced together the peril of nuclear holocaust
and have reaffirmed our faith in the possibility of
    peace.
As we have struggled from our sleep,
we have seen our city and our country
slumbering on in the deepening shadow
cast over our world by the mushroom cloud.
Yet, the hope presented by the resurrection
has enlightened our hearts and broken
the bonds which have held us all entombed.

Our resurrection response
is a passionate commitment to peace
through all the nonviolent means which belong
to our long Christian tradition.

We will fast, pray, organize, and act.
• We will do all we can to make
  Canada's co-operation in the nuclear arms race
  a major issue in the 1984 federal election.
• We will urge our government to stop
  using the tax dollars of Canadian citizens
  to subsidize companies producing nuclear arms.
  We will offer our human energies to Litton Industries
  in a co-operative search for ways in which
  they can profitably return
  to the manufacture of peaceful products.

- On Pentecost Sunday, we will go to Ottawa
  to express our support
  for MPS who promote peace
  and to question those who are trying to legitimate
  the arms race through legislation.
- That same day we will begin to send forth
  some of our members in pairs to capitals
  of those countries engaged in preparations
  for a global holocaust. We will go
  to Moscow, to Washington, and to the capitals
  of Western and Eastern Bloc nations.
  We will ask representatives of these governments
  to stop, in the name of God, in the name of humanity,
  their participation in preparing a nuclear war.

This Easter morning,
we commit ourselves to a relentless resistance
against the forces of darkness and death
which have shrouded minds with the naive hope
of social salvation through nuclear arms.
We believe that our earth's security
lies — not in weapons —
but in justice and equity for all
regardless of race, creed, class, colour, or sex.
We affirm that our country
is called to be a peaceable kingdom,
not an outpost of empires
toying with global destruction.
We deny that our country is doomed
to complicity in mass murder by co-operating
in the production and testing of the cruise missile.
Fifty years ago, Christians slumbered in silence
as Hitler executed the holocaust of the Jewish people.
We will not now stand by while the holocaust
of the human race is being prepared in our midst.

Today we join with Christians and with all people
of good will everywhere
in casting off quiet despair.

Peace is dawning in our world.

*May 1983*
With the announcement that our peace group is willing
to take letters to Moscow and Washington, the mail has
been pouring in. The ones from the children get to me
most. You don't really see the horror of it all until you
see with their eyes. It's the children who keep me from
going numb.

I like life without these darn bombs. If you test these
Arms over here, it could kill both you and I. Why do
you have to test them here? Why do you have to test
them at all. Nobody's perfect. Who cares how big you
bomb is. What if it all of a sudden bloes up? Then
we would all be dead. Remember accident do happen. And in the Bible, Peace on earth, Good will
toward others, is the rule.
    So come on, give us proud Canadians a break and
forget about the bombs.

Jerry Lorette

I think that you guys shouldn't destroy the world.
Why would you want to destroy the world after all
the work you put into it. Plus, why would you want
to destroy the world that God made.

Pat Pelletier

My name is Steven. I have one little brother who is
two years old. I also have a three year old sister and

a seven year old sister. I am the oldest one. I am nine years old. I am planning to be a artist when I grow up. If you read this letter plese don't have world war 3, for the sake of all of us and so my little brother and sisters grow up.

Stephen R. Lafrenière

I don't think we should have wars because I would like to grow up to be a healthy man. But if two countries have a little bit of misunderstanding about islands they have wars. I think they should sit down and talk about it because if they have a war and were in it we might not be their tomorrow to tell about it. If you have a sport like me I like hockey you wouldn't be able to play it any more and you can't see your parents any more that would be pretty sad. So my point is to use your heads and not your weapons.

Darren Kaus

### THE VIEW FROM THE QUEEN STREET CAR
### (TS, May 14, 1983)

Notes made on the Queen St. streetcar while on the way to work:

We wait for the streetcar in the morning, shivering and solitary. The clothes are Honest Ed's, Towers, and vintage Goodwill.

We get on. I sit next to a man somewhere between sleeping and waking. A permanent state of being for so many along this street...sleepwalking. I look out of the window at Plato's Burgers. Like all the other 24-hour spots along this route — full. It is warm inside — like the streetcar. It is home.

Going shopping...going to school. A few of us going to

work. Most just going. At Brock St. a man weaves onto the car. Smells of everything and nothing. People shuffle around him. He has his problems—we have ours.

The women are made up—too much or too little. You gotta pay to look natural. Lot of carrot-coloured hair.... We move slowly past the run-down stores for put-down people.

We stop at Queen St. Mental Health Centre. A man with a coat and leather briefcase gets on. Maybe a doctor from the night shift. Looks cool but seems worn. Over-worked. His problem—the flip side of the flop houses around here.

Another man gets on. Grinning. "I'm going to Number 10 Downing!" Little smiles break out around him. We've grown to like these "crazies". We can all stop pretending it makes sense.

A woman gets on with baby. Her face is the morning world. The old man across beams.

At Niagara St. the cleaners and seamstresses get on. They will drop off again around Spadina and scurry down the street. They will drag on again about five p.m. They have to work; their husbands don't make enough. They have to get home to cook, to clean, to care. Each day they grey.

St. Christopher House, the Harbour Light Centre, Brother's Clothing Store...at Beverley St. the punkers get on. Black eyes on white faces on black clothes. The war against beige.

The Grange, Osgoode Hall, City Hall, Bay St., Simpsons. The secretaries, the clerks, and the waitresses get off.

The lawyers, the politicians, and the businessmen do not get on or off. They drive cars to work. And listen to the news with the latest figures about unemployment. And listen to music.

At Victoria St. the woman sits over the hot air vent outside the drug store. She sits—all day, all night. They all sit—outside Metropolitan United Church, Moss Park Armoury. Or stand—along the walls of Church and Jarvis and Sherbourne.

Pawnshops. Fred Victor Mission, Good Shepherd Refuge, army surplus stores...and the sandblasted shops that cater to the blow-dried people.

I get off and go to work. The streetcar goes on. Every day it goes on. People get off and on and off and on. The Humber-Neville circle of quiet despair. My daily meditation on the state of the economy.

*June 1983*

Paul Robinson was sentenced June 20 for theft of over half a million dollars from money intended for the poor (Development and Peace). This may or may not be the end of our campaign. Surely people will see that he could only do what he did because of the secrecy surrounding the financial decisions at Sharelife.

According to the evidence at the brief, very brief trial, he spent most of the money on gambling trips—fifty-six in one year. He would have been away from the city most of the time—and he wasn't. I went to see the Crown prosecutor to ask him why he hadn't pursued the question of where the money was spent and by whom. He just smiled obscurely: "The cardinal has friends in high places."

*July 1983*

I let my name stand for election in our community and it happened. It is going to mean far less time at *Catholic New Times* but I'm willing to do this for the community. Most of who I have become is because of my community. And I believe in what we are about, and in what women religious are about. I've seen at *Catholic New Times* how they are the ones who are always willing to take the risk of new and small beginnings.

One of my first responsibilities was to go to the meeting of the heads of religious communities in the States, in Baltimore. It was quite a meeting as the Vatican had just issued a statement on "The Essential Elements of Religious Life". I was impressed by the women there and the clarity with which they spoke. They know what they believe in and they are not willing to equate loyalty to the church with just following the orders of the Vatican.

*September 1983*
The delegation from our peace group* was supposed to leave for Moscow with the letters from the children when we heard the news that the Korean jetliner had been shot down. It is a tense moment. Should we go? All of the airlines have stopped traffic in and out of Moscow — except the one we are booked on, Swissair. But will we get out if we go? We've prayed about this together and decided that now more than ever we need to go. For the first time in my life I made sure someone knew where my will was.

*Monday September 12* It's hard to know if the weather is clouding our outlook. As we rode into Moscow we saw a grey city with block after block of dreary apartment complexes which seemed to hold eight million inhabitants silently captive.

*Tuesday 13* We go to a reception at the Canadian embassy.

---

* The Christian Initiative for Peace delegation to Moscow included: Mrs. Dierdre McLoughlin, the Very Rev. Clarke MacDonald, Rev. Cliff Elliott, Fr. Paul Hansen c.ss.r., Rev. John Hess, and Sr. Mary Jo Leddy. A second delegation went to Washington at the same time.

Geoffrey Pearson, the ambassador, is obviously conscious of all the nuances in the context. As I begin to introduce myself, he interrupts and says he's already heard a lot about me from the "reports". I am a little unnerved at the thought that I have entered some information system on national security. This is hardball politics. Later I am outraged about the surveillance of good citizens in the name of "democracy".

*Wednesday 14* Three-hour ordeal session with the official Soviet peace committee in the afternoon. They are very defensive because of bad experiences on their recent Canadian trip. They lecture us for an hour and a half on why America is most responsible for the arms race. Cliff Elliott makes a valiant effort to shift the ground of the discussion to common human concerns. We fail. No dialogue except perhaps in the sincere handshakes at the end. Did they have to say all that? Are our two reporters KGB? We all agreed that this "official" group isn't a credible voice for peace.

We start a night watch over the phone. The *Toronto Star* will be calling through at three a.m. The reporter there relays the news that the Washington group had a hard day...were called Communists. Here we're called agents of capitalism.

*Thursday 15* Today we met a smiling Russian prophet! After a three-hour search through the maze of Moscow, John Hess, Deirdre McLoughlin, and I found the apartment of Yuri Medvedkov, the chief spokesperson for the independent peace group. He's fifty-three, a geologist. Scattered around the living room were many of the books we were familiar with: Jonathan Schell's *The Fate of the Earth*, Robert Jay Lifton's *Indefensible Weapons*. We learned quickly that the apartment is bugged but, to our surprise, Yuri spoke openly about the activities of the group. We only used the erasable pad to write the times of future meetings. He gave us a statement on the tragedy of flight KAL007 and asked us to publicize it. Quite similar to our statement: "The absence of trust between the two superpowers is the killer." Yuri told us that the group had become vulnerable since KAL007 because its contacts with the West had been cut off with the stopping of flights to Moscow. Begged us to tell peace activists to continue to come and see the group. Talked about KGB harassment of the group in recent days and asked us to speak of this. "Publicity is our only protection now." This group isn't really "dissident". They want to work within Soviet law to show the strong desire for peace among ordinary Russians.

We learned that Yuri and his wife, Olga, are *refuseniks* — Jews who have applied to emigrate to Israel, whose request has been refused by the Soviet government. I left a ring I was wearing for Olga. Mom brought it back from Israel last year. The Hebrew inscription reads "Jerusalem", the City of Peace. The ring belonged with Olga.

*Friday 16* Five of us kept the second appointment with Yuri at his apartment. He told us more about the history of the group and their recent difficulties with the KGB: phones cut, wives hassled, members followed, arrests, some members shipped out of Moscow. What of the future? "In these weeks we face dangers. Local hawks are using this moment to do away with us. They may crush us individually but they cannot crush the desire for peace among the people." We were humbled. He invited us to a "peace seminar" at his place at seven p.m. that night.

After that, things moved quickly. We returned to find a note from Clarke MacDonald saying the Canadian embassy had arranged an appointment for him with a high-level Kremlin official who would receive our letters. He had had to leave without us. Then Cliff, Deirdre, and John went to meet with a peace representative of the Orthodox church. They were to meet me later at Yuri's. Paul Hansen stayed to meet Clarke.

I made it to Yuri's well before seven. It was the evening of Yom Kippur. Gathered in the small room were the non-religious Jews and the Christians in the group. There was a mood of apprehension. We had water and almonds.

The evening became stop-frame—each face clearly focused for ever in my memory. Yuri, Olga—passionate and practical. Beautiful Marsha, an engineer who was five months pregnant. Igor, a psychiatrist with the face of a Russian mystic. Valery, lanky and gentle, a physicist who had lost his job—as had Mark, the mathematician. They knew, I knew, that they could soon be in a "mental hospital", their brains turned to mush. I shuddered at the price of it all.

There was an American peace group in town that was expected to come. They didn't show. Neither did the others from our group. We began the seminar anyway. It was given by Lev Dudkin, unemployed economist. His topic: the conversion of companies from the production of arms to the production of socially useful products. I mentioned our efforts to get Litton in Toronto to do just that. They were very excited about this and promised to have a proposal for Litton to consider ready by the next day. I was to meet them at the synagogue during the Yom Kippur service to get the proposal. Yuri gave me a tape recording of the seminar and copies of the group's statements to governments and peace activists in the West.

There was a knock at the door during the seminar. Yuri and Olga had forty-eight hours to report for two months' research duty on the Caspian Sea.

As I left, Olga stopped me and asked me, "Have you

ever been to Jerusalem?" I told her I had. "Tell me what it is like." A thousand images flashed through my mind but only one seemed important. "When you drive up to Jerusalem in the spring," I said, "you can smell the orange blossoms everywhere." She breathed that in. "I will remember." It was something to hope on, something as real as the smell of orange blossoms in the spring.

Years before, I had gone to Israel because I wanted to. I had no idea, until that moment with Olga, what that visit could mean for others beyond myself. Now I knew. It was all for this one moment — to share the aroma of hope with someone who had little reason to hope.

I left the apartment and made my way to the subway. As I looked behind, I saw two men following me. Were they KGB? Too many John le Carré novels, Mary Jo! Yet there was too much at stake to treat this as fiction — I had the tapes and documents in my jacket. I raced through the subway stations, switching trains for an hour until the two men were nowhere to be seen.

When I finally returned to our group at the hotel, I heard of the events of the past few hours. The KGB had told Paul and Clarke that we "were engaging in activities contrary to the best interests of the Soviet Union because we were affiliating with people who were committing acts against the Soviet government." We were told not to see the peace group or make phone calls to the West. We were to be good tourists or else. Cliff reported that he, Deirdre, and John had been blocked from entering Yuri's apartment by KGB agents stationed at the entrance. It appears I arrived too early to meet them.

What to do? We agreed that the best thing we could do was to concentrate on getting the tape recording (which we want to get to Litton), films, and notes out of there. Then we could tell their story.

*Saturday 17 (Yom Kippur)* We went over to the synagogue on Archipova St. What a sight on that little side street! The atmosphere of the Day of Atonement was far from sombre. Hundreds of Jews milled outside the synagogue, taking advantage of a break in the service to exchange information. We mixed with them and talked with several young *refuseniks*. One of them told me that Yuri, Olga, and the others had been picked up that morning.

We went into the synagogue to pray — that we all might turn from evil to good. As I looked at the old man in front of me with the tattered prayer shawl, I realized that he was reading the Hebrew text with his finger from left to right instead of from right to left. He didn't know what he was reading at all, but he was being faithful in the only way he knew.

*Sunday 18* Being good tourists...we went for an afternoon walk in the park. We were followed by our KGB shadows. Everything and everyone was bathed in sunlight. Children laughed by the fountains, lovers walked hand in hand, friends shared some secret story, and the elderly patiently watched it all from their privileged places on park benches. How impossible it was then to think of all these people being erased with one of our nuclear bombs. Would that they could see Nathan Phillips Square and High Park and all our other people places. Then the thought of dropping a bomb on our city would become unimaginable for them.

We went over to the Canadian embassy. I refused to leave until I had the assurance that the tape and documents would be put in a diplomatic pouch to Canada.

We strategized as to how to get my diary through the search at Customs, assuming the KGB knew I had been with the independent peace group. Deirdre offered to put the pages in her bra and girdle. Cliff observed that she wore the biblical "breastplate of honour" and had "girded her loins with truth"!

*December 1983*
Another trip. This time to Honduras, in a hastily-put-together effort to have women religious go on a prayer pilgrimage to the U.S. military bases on the Honduran-Nicaraguan border.

We never got there. The plane was stopped on the tarmac, surrounded by armed soldiers, and sent back to Miami. What does it say about the state of things when praying becomes such a dangerous political activity?

Was most struck by the remarks of Congresswoman Pat Shroeder (D-Colorado) in the subsequent press conference. Once again struck by the difference between those who hold fast to the founding ideals of the republic and those who have imperialistic dreams for the American empire.

Her remarks as she sat surrounded by the American nuns: "They are involved in a rescue mission, perhaps not quite as dramatic as the one in the Caribbean, but a rescue mission none the less. They will rescue the U.S. from its militaristic folly in Central America. I say will rescue because they will do it. Here in Washington and out in their communities—they will do it. Barring them from Honduras will not stop their mission.... We are faced with a 'hear no evil, see no evil' administration. It wants to shroud the press; destroy the independent Civil Rights Commission; veto the human rights certification process. Here in this hemisphere and elsewhere, it has replaced the shining beacon of the Statue of Liberty with an M-16 rifle. But that is not America. America is here in this room."

Three of us Canadians went on to Ottawa to inform parliamentarians about what had happened. Most serious was the fact that we were not allowed to speak to any representative of the Canadian embassy. If that is acceptable, then it bodes ill for Canadian missionaries working in Honduras.

After we had finished talking with the NDP caucus, Father Bob Ogle (NDP-Saskatoon) took me for lunch in the parliamentary dining room. The prime minister walked by and Bob stopped him. "This is Sister Mary Jo Leddy, and she and several other sisters were stopped from entering Honduras by armed soldiers." Brian Mulroney smiled mellifluously: "Do pray for me, sister." The mouth in search of meaning.

*New Year's Day, 1984*
I think we are all feeling somewhat besieged. Last night we seemed like such a little group. Holdouts. The conservatives seem to be on a roll—in the church and in the governments. And it seems clear that the conservatives are growing in power because many people agree with them. There is a not-so-blessed rage for order.

Why are people so anxious to defend God and the church? Is their faith in God and the church so weak that they think it will all fall apart if they don't prop it up?

From Peru, Luigi writes that the new bishop in his area belongs to Opus Dei. Luigi's days are probably numbered. The rector of Mark's seminary told him that Mark's activities were bad publicity for the place—especially the front-page photo of Mark being dragged out of the senator's office. Ann's application for tenure was derailed because of a feminist article she wrote. Jim told us he would probably have to resign because he could no longer tolerate the mayor's racist agenda. Bill is increasingly frustrated because his most creative policy papers are being shelved by the assistant deputy minister. And Isabel is out of favour with her dean because she objected to a donation to the college from a union-busting mining company. In the sixties, this would all have been rather socially acceptable.

As for me, I know my phone is tapped and the files in my office have been ransacked — probably because of the ongoing meetings of Christian Initiative for Peace. We are gearing up for an action on Ash Wednesday.

The saving grace — to be able to laugh together at all of this. Isabel did a marvellous imitation of her twitchy little dean. Mark weighed the pros and cons of dressing up or dressing down for a sit-in. The power that comes from pooh-poohing! And we laughed at ourselves as well, flakes that we sometimes are. Confessed we'd rather eat a big greasy hamburger than go vegetarian, could easily become beach bums on some third-world shore, would love to hear more Gregorian chant.

Yes — a saving grace. Most groups I'm involved with can't even entertain the possibility of self-criticism. Could be fatal. Feeling besieged, we become more critical of what is "out there". We become rigid in our approach, unable to shift to more effective strategies.

Bill and Susan brought their new baby — a healthy girl named Ann. A saving grace.


### THE BOMB MAY DEADEN US BEFORE IT DROPS
(TS, Jan. 28, 1984)

It is called "nuclearism". According to Yale professor Robert Jay Lifton, it is the psychological syndrome of the nuclear age.

Nuclearism affects any normal person and yet results in the most serious abnormalities. Its symptoms are psychological and even religious and yet its cure must, in the end, be social and political.

Lifton has described the syndrome of nuclearism in his latest book, *Indefensible Weapons*. It is a study with far-reaching implications which can be ignored only at our own peril.

Referring to recent American psychological studies, Lifton concludes that we are all living with deep and inarticulate fears of nuclear extinction — fears which are intensified rather than extinguished by the nuclear arms race. Such feelings are as taboo in our age as sexual feelings were in a previous time, he says. As long as we are unable to alleviate our nuclear fears in any practical way, we will continue to repress those fears. A process of deep freezing begins which then has a numbing effect on all our feelings — about ourselves, about others, about God. This is the numbness of nuclearism, and it is a normal reaction to the realities of our times.

Human beings were not created to cope with the holocaust of millions of people in half an hour. Our minds and hearts were not created to grasp such a monstrous possibility. We cannot think of the vaporization of one person, much less a whole city. Our hearts and our minds were made for so much less — and so much more — than this.

So...we bury ourselves in business as usual. We force ourselves to forget that the unthinkable has become the possible.

Lifton points out that, even though the repression of our fears of the future is a normal reaction in a nuclear age, it results in a serious psychological perversion in the present. Not only does the arms race deprive the poor of their physical health, it also robs us all of our psychological health. Is it any wonder that so many eat, drink, and are merry when they suspect that tomorrow they may perish?

Witness the rush to consume before we are consumed, the need for the numbing effects of alcohol and drugs, the collapse of long-term commitments to people and projects, the flight from reality into warm and fuzzy religion.

There are other, less obvious symptoms of nuclearism. Mindless activism can be a race from the thought of the world stopping. Cool professionalism can be an insulation against the burning questions of the day. Single-issue concerns can be a refuge from the fact that everything is now at issue.

Religion itself can become a casualty of this nuclearism — even if the button is never pushed. Why? Because religion can only dabble in the present, without giving direction to it, if there are no deep questions about the future for religion to respond to.

The god of nuclearism becomes a frozen reality, an idolatrous projection of our desperate attempt to control the fears within. Yet authentic religion can also become the antifreeze that reverses the process of nuclear numbing. The central belief of the Judeo-Christian tradition is that there is no fear so deep that it cannot be encompassed by an even deeper hope.

Lifton says that we need to see models of people who have faced the fears of nuclear destruction without being overwhelmed by them, so that we ourselves can move beyond the paralysis of nuclearism. He does not discuss how or why such personal change takes place.

I believe that only religious faith moves us to enter the tomb of our nuclear despair — the only place where the fullness of fear and hope begins to rise within us.

However painful a process that may be, it is more life-giving than the attempt to bury those fears.

The nuclear bomb will deaden us all before it drops if we allow our numbness in the face of its reality to continue. Our fears must be enlivened by hope if they are to direct our action for peace.

*February 1984*

It began as just another talk on peace at the University Women's Club. Then this somewhat stylish woman came up to me after the talk and said, "I am the woman on the Queen Street car." After the article in the *Toronto Star* on the Queen Street car I had received an anonymous letter from a woman who said she spent most of her time in a doughnut shop. She had lost her job and was living on welfare. "You would probably never recognize me as one of those depressed people on the streetcar," she had written. I had reprinted the letter in my column with the intention of raising the awareness of the readers.

"I was hurt that you reprinted my letter," she said. "It was for you — not for the world."

I had nothing to say. I felt as if I had violated her trust, used her for some political purpose. Am I becoming like what I am fighting against? Are people becoming projects, objects of concern for me?

She was a messenger.

### CALCIFIED CHAOS
#### (TS, Feb. 25, 1984)

There is a rage for order which is all the rage these days. This rage rails between the lines of Ronald Reagan's recent budget and pours out in letters to the editor of a publication such as the *Star*.

Many of the churches have hoisted their sails to catch this raging wind. In the Catholic church it has become fashionable to say that the time of Vatican II is over. Those who say this usually mean that what they see as a time of unbridled change and chaos is over.

For the sake of brevity (but at the risk of simplification) let us say that this concern for order comes from the conservative element in society and in the churches. And let us infer from the writings of many conservatives that they see liberals as dreaded agents of disorder.

I sympathize with the concern of reasonable and responsible conservatives for order. One has only to talk with parents who see their children caught in a crossfire of conflicting social signals to know the anguish which gives rise to the desire for at least a few sure points of reference.

One has only to meet with enough liberals to know that the conservatives' caricature of them is a little accurate: liberals who froth at the mouth are often, well, flaky.

Yet, while I respect a reasonable conservativism, I am appalled by a raging conservativism. It leaves you with the taste of vinegar. It exposes you to the pornography of pettiness. It incites you to riot or repression.

It is interesting to note that the rage of the conservative bears a startling resemblance to the rage of the liberal. The one rages for order while the other rages for disorder — but the worlds they want are only mirror images of each other. And both worlds are, in my opinion, founded on a flawed notion of what order is.

The problem with raging conservatives is not their fear of freedom but their faulty sense of order. What many conservatives call order is nothing more than calcified chaos.

We do not live in an ordered society. In my estimation, we live in a society radically disordered by poverty and injustice. Only a reordering of social relationships will remove the causes of disruption in the social order. Believing conservatives, however, want to control the chaos of injustice in our society through rigid laws and unbending structures.

A similar dynamic takes place in the churches. Consider some of the disruptions in the Roman Catholic Church which conservatives seek to contain through the calcification process of repeated pronouncements.

The chaos of injustice is only barely contained. Pity the poor women who suggest that something is the matter with the order of a church that always puts them in second place. The women will inevitably be called "disorderly elements".

These women will not rest in peace. "Peace," wrote Saint Thomas Aquinas, "is the tranquillity of order."

*February 1984*

We've been standing outside Litton Industries for a few days now. Thought it would only be a few hours before we could meet the president of the company and present him with the recommendations of the independent peace group in Moscow. He won't come out and so in some foolish, outrageous, and spirit-driven decision we have decided to stay until he comes.

The cold is bone-numbing. We are scrambling to get the clothes we need and some cars to sleep in at night. I keep thinking of Olga and Yuri in Moscow – it's the least we can do.

Most difficult is going to the bathroom. We go down the road to the Skyline Hotel to use the john, but have to pass through the swimming pool area (*cum* sauna) in the process. The seductive power of that warm swimming pool is overwhelming. Would love to fall into the warmth and stay there for ever.

En route to the washroom there is also a telephone. Try to connect to keep up my commitments to the paper, to my community, and to the rest of the world. Meanwhile, the hotel is hosting an exhibit on the uses of tofu!

We are out here, strangely out of time and out of place. It is as if everything has stopped for us and we are here – waiting in the little strip of land between the roadway and the fence of Litton Industries. The security cameras scan us back and forth, back and forth.

We know this much, we can count on each other. After all those early morning meetings we know some of us will always be there, to pray together, to deliver food, to find the tent that we need to sleep in.

The cold has been brutal. My face, like the faces of others, is swollen, and our lips are blistered from the battering wind. Yet it is such a blessed time. There is nothing we can do but be together, be somehow with the mysterious reality of it all. Friends have come out to visit us and we've had the time together that we've never had in years. And I've had hours to walk along City View Drive and just pray about the road that has led me thus far. My most political action has provided me with a most contemplative moment. The cold has brought its own crystal clarity about where I am and why.

THE CHOSEN LIFE

(CNT, Feb. 26, 1984)

"To whom shall we go?" "Where do you live?" "Who do you say I am?" These are the questions born somewhere between the marrow and the bone. They are the questions of the heart which emerge from that mysterious centre where we are who we are.

Questions of the heart are not easily answered but they can, none the less, be lived with and responded to. Without these questions our lives shrivel on the surface and narrow into nothingness.

We ask these questions only because God is in quest of us. We seek because we have already been found, founded, in God. Our response to these questions will determine with whom we cast our lot, where we draw the line, how we count our blessings.

There are times when we live these questions with greatness of heart, with boldness and delicacy of spirit. But there are other times when we answer too quickly — or too slowly.

Real commitment begins when the heart is broken open by love. Our hearts may be passionate, frail, or tender, but until they are broken open by love, we cannot be committed.

In love one becomes compelled and free, driven and desiring. In love, the difference between choosing and being chosen dissolves.

It is almost impossible to explain or deny commitments of the heart. Everything is explained in love, but love itself cannot be explained. How does a man explain why he wants to marry this woman and no other? How does a priest explain why he can yawn happily on a Sunday evening after a week of ministering to the living dead? How does a sister explain why she has sold everything for the privilege of living among the poor? How does a neighbour explain why she keeps dropping in on an old friend who no longer recognizes her? How does a seminarian explain why he thinks he can live without sex and not die in the process? How does a mother explain why she prefers diapers and dirt to a kid-free condominium?

Only those who live in love know why.

Commitment is not a matter of dogged determination or ferocious acts of the will. It is the way life is chosen when love takes over.

However, our hearts are sometimes unfaithful to the way of love that is ours — we fritter away our faith, hobble our hope, overplay our passion.

Ultimately such commitment is possible because God

is present in the heart of the world — a faithfully loving God who is greater than our hearts.

We say words like "for ever" and "for better or worse" when we discover the heart of another person or when we suddenly touch the core of what has been just an issue. We can say "yes" and "amen" when we put on the heart of Christ.

## *March 1984*

Drove in from Litton to meet with Bob Ogle. He is in the midst of his own vigil. The Vatican has nixed his effort to continue as a priest-politician in Parliament. His face was almost purple as we sat there in our community room. I worried about the toll that all of this was taking. What a long way it has been for both of us, I thought, from the simpler and clearer life we knew on the prairies. I first met him when I was a high-school student and he was the rector of the seminary in Saskatoon. Our project was to design a mural for the outside of the Catholic Centre there. We wanted something that sang of golden wheat, of long sky and never-ending light.

And now we are both groping in a dimly lit world, in a dark and shadowed church.

### THE ROBERTO PROJECT
#### (CNT, March 25, 1984)

For hours he had been tossing and turning. He had until morning to make up his mind about accepting the political nomination. Unable to sleep, he left the rectory and went over to the church to pray.

The sun began to dawn but Father Robert Ogle felt plunged in darkness. In desperation, he made the decision to take his cue from the breviary reading of that morning.

The gospel of the day commanded, "Do not hide your light under a bushel."

It was done. The night of agony was over but he was left with only a profound feeling of sadness.

The priest recalls the feeling of loss that accompanied his decision to enter politics. "I got up from the pew and walked down the aisle to the door. I knew that once I walked out of that door I would never be safe again. I would always be marked as the political priest." He opened the door and walked into the cold morning air.

That was seven years ago. Now that door seems to be closed. A February 21 letter from the Vatican has withdrawn the permission Fr. Ogle had to enter the world of politics.

There are those on Parliament Hill who would say that, during his time, Fr. Ogle forced the government to open its doors to the concerns of the churches. Through his membership in interparliamentary committees on Latin America and disarmament, Ogle raised moral issues which would otherwise have remained dormant. With clarity and consistency, he argued from a pro-life position — defending human life from the moment of conception to death. His fellow NDPers could only respect his decision to abstain from the vote on the Constitution because it did not guarantee the rights of the unborn.

Talk to politicians of any stripe in Ottawa and you will hear the wide respect in which Ogle is held. They know he has the talent to become the leader of any party but they know that is not his purpose in being in Ottawa. They tell stories of how Ogle says his daily mass even during high-powered international meetings when there does not seem to be a minute to lose.

Bob Ogle has never defined the role of a priest-politician. He has described it through his action. This was "the

Roberto project", which a group of contemplative nuns in Bolivia had prayed for.

He met these nuns during a year-long trip around the world in 1975-76. He almost died in the jungle before he made it to the Benedictine monastery in the Alto Plato of Bolivia. While he was recuperating, he told the sisters of his uncertainty regarding what he would do when he returned to the diocese of Saskatoon. As he was leaving the monastery, the superior told him the community would pray that he would find what he was meant to do — the "Roberto project".

He returned to Saskatoon and within a few months he was asked to let his name stand for the NDP nomination in Saskatoon East.

The sisters had understood how he had been touched by his years as a missionary in Brazil and by his travels throughout the third world. They knew he needed a project that would help him serve the needs of the people he had met.

Has the "Roberto project" come to an end? Something has. The letter to Ogle from the Vatican suggests that a dispensation from the rule regarding priests in politics is not possible at this time.

Ogle briefly considered appealing his case, and would have been supported by his bishop in this effort. In the process of weighing the pros and cons of such an attempt, Ogle contacted his "tunnel community". These are the people who, as he explains, "are with me no matter where I am. They are back there even when I am out in front and there is no light."

It was a conversation with his sister Mary Lou, a no-nonsense person who directs his office in Saskatoon, which turned him away from the avenue of appeal. She told him he would never feel right if he started to bargain with the Vatican. "You would be like Oliver begging outside the door to get something more," she said. His mind was made up.

Ogle returned to Saskatoon to prepare to make the announcement of his resignation at the annual meeting of his riding association on March 1. He returned home to the prairies, to the big sky and the horizon that makes everything seem more relative. There are those who say Saskatoon was not big enough for Robert Ogle, and there are others who know Ottawa was too small for him.

In the days before the meeting, he tried to carry on as usual. He flew up to Meadow Lake to speak at a nomination meeting for Doug Anguish. The pilot of the small private plane told Ogle the story of why he was a socialist even though he owned eighty quarters of land. "In 1933 my mother had a gallstone attack but the local hospital wouldn't let her in because she couldn't pay seventeen dollars. She died and I've been a socialist ever since."

Ogle thought about that as he looked down at the flat land dotted with signs of the toeholds of human life. His first assignment in Parliament had been to act as health critic for the NDP.

Fog kept the plane from returning to Saskatoon that evening. At midnight, Ogle and his pilot were wandering around North Battleford looking for a motel room. It was difficult to sleep because the motel had been taken over by what seemed like all the teenagers in the province, who were in town for a broomball tournament.

Ogle got up early and bundled off down the street to a local greasy spoon for breakfast. As he sipped his coffee, he listened to the conversations in the booths around him. A group of three men were agonizing over where to bowl that day. And he was agonizing over how to drop the bombshell about his resignation. Different people, different struggles.

He gave a talk at Holy Cross High School about how

the gospel is to be lived in a global village. He knew he was off. "I was uptight — too loud and hard."

One student asked, with cultivated cynicism, about the possibility of social change. "One saint is worth five million selfish people in the area of social change," he answered, and then turned to address the student directly. "You're selfish now but you can become saints — if you choose."

The night of the general meeting finally arrived. Perhaps significantly, it was held at St. Philip's, a school in the parish where Ogle had served before his election.

The candidate rose to address the audience. There was a stunned silence when he told them of his decision to resign. He recalled that, at his nomination acceptance speech in 1977, he had stated his intention to remain a priest "before, during, and after my involvement in politics."

Some of the Catholics at the meeting were loud in their anger. Shocked and surprised, they felt all the bases had been covered with the Vatican.

A man called Jim Wild spoke up. "We talk a lot about you at work, Father. You taught us how to live religion, not just on Sunday but all through the week." They stood and clapped fifteen minutes for Bob Ogle. It had been a class act from start to finish.

Ogle had done everything possible to avoid this moment. He had been assured twice by the Vatican that he could continue in politics with his bishop's permission. The Bishop of Saskatoon, James P. Mahoney, had approved. Not without difficulty, not without doubts — but once he had given his priest permission, he backed him all the way.

Bishop Mahoney and Fr. Ogle had been together in the seminary but their paths had gone in different directions. Mahoney had spent years working in high schools and marriage counselling. Ogle had been a seminary rector, a marriage tribunal judge, and a chancellor. He was a young priest on his way up the hierarchical ladder – until he went to Latin America.

In Brazil, he realized that governments had to change if the poor of this world were to be fed and clothed. The poor eventually led him to politics, to the "Roberto project".

The project has ended. Roberto may be just beginning.

## *April 1984*

We have been here outside Litton for thirty-one days. I had almost decided to stay here for months if necessary, but we received word that the Etobicoke city council had received a complaint about our little tent as a "health hazard" and had ordered us off the public property of the city. We decided to take advantage of the order and to appeal to city council for the right to retain our position on the four-foot strip of land that lies in front of Litton Industries. In our opinion, Litton is the real health hazard.

The meeting with the city council was on April 9, and what an interesting lot they are. We made our case well, although rather feebly in some ways. I could barely speak because of my throat infection, and blood dripped down my chin every time I smiled – cold sores. In the end, it seemed that pity and not reason prevailed. Mayor Dennis Flynn said he thought it was terrible that "Sister" and all the others were left out in the cold – and he offered to negotiate a meeting with Ronald Keating, the head of Litton Industries.

So I met with Ron Keating and Dennis Flynn on April 30. I said what I had to say and tried to tell them about those people in Moscow who were working for peace as much as we were. And Keating said what he had to say. And that was all.

And has all of this, all of these days and nights shivering, made any difference? I don't know, may never know.

### THE HOLY SATURDAY PEOPLE
#### (TS, April 24, 1984)

Some people clean house, others cook up a storm. Some make up for lost time, others put in time.

It's that awkward time between the gloom of Good Friday and the surprise of Easter Sunday. Few are content to take Holy Saturday on its own terms.

That's unfortunate. In my opinion, an examination of our experience of Holy Saturday reveals a great deal about the meaning of human life. Most of our human experience falls in that grey area which is neither darkness nor dawn.

The church has long recognized this essentially Holy Saturday quality of our lives in its doctrinal statements. It has rejected any theology that says human experience is only darkness or only light: it has called "heretical" any interpretation (such as that put forth by the Manicheans) that says life is a struggle between two distinct forces of light and darkness. Yet the denials of the Holy Saturday nature of human life are still with us.

Manicheans, for example, are not in short supply. Listen to President Ronald Reagan line himself up with the forces of light against the total darkness of Communism. Watch some of the TV evangelists draw the line between sinners and the saved—and watch which side of the line they fall on. Read some of the literature of the left and discover a new dogma: "Outside the left there is no salvation."

Christianity, which has endured throughout history in a prolonged period of Holy Saturday, has never completely divided the light from the darkness of human experience.

Authentic Christianity has always said: there is no darkness so dark that it is not broken by some shaft of light, which is the Spirit. Thus, no person, no group, no system, is beyond redemption.

And Christianity has also said: there is no light so bright that it is not diminished by the shadow of sin. Thus, there is no person or situation which can claim the security of salvation. Christianity has followed a path which has avoided the extremes of despair or presumption because there have always been enough people who have lived out the mystery of Holy Saturday in their human experience.

Holy Saturday people do not despair of themselves or of others: they do not give up on the possibility of change. On the other hand, Holy Saturday people do not presume very much. They don't take God or others for granted. They know the sand that a sense of security is built on. They don't throw stones because they know they are not without sin themselves.

Holy Saturday people know that there are two choices to be made in the time of one's life: the decision to accept death and the decision to choose life. And they know those two choices are not the same choice.

Holy Saturday people — some may call them "together" and others may call them "realistic" but I would call them hopeful. They wear well. They wait well.

### THE LIBERATION OF THE MIDDLE CLASS
(CNT, May 6, 1984)

In the early seventies, I was captivated by the theology of liberation which was emerging in Latin America. Through some university classes and personal contact with people from the third world, I started to get a feel for the key insights of this new theology. I learned that justice and charity were two different, although not unrelated, responses which one could make to the problem of poverty. I became aware of how one responded to the symptoms of poverty through charity and how one addressed the causes of that poverty by working to change the social structures that perpetuated such misery. I understood how any theology that kept our eyes fixed on heaven alone would serve to justify the status quo of the earthly reality in Latin America — a reality in which the rich get richer and the poor get poorer.

In such an extreme situation of wealth and poverty, it seemed clear that those who were not with the poor were against them. An option had to be made. In Latin America, middle ground morality was, and is, an illusion.

The theology of liberation gave me a new insight into the reality of God and human experience because it was a theology that shared in the angle of vision of the poor.

It was around this time that a group of us got together and laid the groundwork for the founding of *Catholic New Times*. It began with the desire to give a voice to the struggling efforts at liberation which were taking place within the church community. We felt it was important for people here in Canada to hear about the struggles for justice elsewhere.

However, as the months and years went by, as *Catholic New Times* began to take shape, I took note of some rather uncomfortable facts I read in the letters to the editor, facts I also heard from various groups as I travelled around the country. I had to face the fact that the intense concern for social justice which so animated our newspaper seldom went beyond the circle of the "already committed".

The "committed", more often than not, were those who had travelled to some third-world country and had formed personal bonds of solidarity with the people there. But most of the people in the Canadian church had not had such an experience, nor were they likely to have it in the future.

For a while, I thought the message of social justice was falling on deaf ears because we were not speaking loudly enough. And I did try screaming. Then I wondered whether the lack of hearing had more to do with hardness of heart or lack of vision. But I had to face the fact that those who seemed so deaf to the call to justice were attentive to many other difficult challenges in their lives.

It was then that I asked myself whether there was something *I* was not hearing.

Some of the ways in which social justice was being presented started to make me uncomfortable: so many educational efforts in the area of justice seemed to rely on guilt as a primary motivation; so many of the talks on liberation theology seemed to rely on a specialized vocabulary that alienated ordinary people; so often the poor seemed to be talked about as objects of concern rather than as people who were cared for.

Then one day an angel came to me with a message I needed to hear. He was the vice-president of a multinational corporation, in his fifties, who did some occasional volunteer work at *Catholic New Times*. He didn't come to our office out of any great commitment to our vision but simply because of some people there whom he had grown to like. He and I had many long discussions about the content of our newspaper. Our coverage of the role of multinationals in the third world was, he felt, quite misguided. In his opinion, these companies were trying to do the best for the people in the third world — in addition to reaping profits for their shareholders.

I told him that much of our information came from missionaries who had seen the devastating effect multinationals had on the lives of people in developing countries.

He dismissed our sources as utterly naive. He had not

seen what the missionaries had seen — haunted eyes, broken backs, the big black boots that enforced the order so necessary for the conduct of good business. He had only seen the nice faces of his fellow executives and the façade of fairness his company had erected about itself.

Then one day he walked into our office and said, "Well, perhaps your sources are right after all, perhaps those multinationals aren't all that fair down there."

I was somewhat stunned by this about-face. He went on to tell me that he had just been fired from his job, fired from the company to which he had given his loyalty for twenty-five years. All of this shortly before his retirement benefits would have gone into effect.

In one moment, he had had an insight into the double-edged reality of the multinational system: the system which had treated him as a disposable commodity could also treat the poor of the third world as grist for its mills.

His anguish gave me a new angle of vision on the need for liberation. His sense of oppression had placed him in immediate solidarity with the oppressed of the third world. Once he knew he was in captivity, he understood the captivity of the poor and could share in their desire for liberation.

It was clear to both of us that the injustice he had experienced had the same systematic source as the injustice being perpetuated in places like Latin America. He knew that the problem was the system, that the same nice people who had fired him in order to survive would soon become disposable too.

This was a man ready to work *with* the poor — not *for* them. It was a revelation to me how the truth of his own situation had enabled him to cross the bridge to the truth of oppression elsewhere. From then on I urged justice educators to spend less time telling the middle class about the oppression of the poor, and more time talking with them about their own need for liberation.

It is a fact that the Canadian Catholic church is a predominantly middle-class church. One statistic (from the Canadian Religious Conference) estimates that 70 per cent of the Roman Catholics in this country are middle class. This is a statistic Karl Marx would never have ignored — given his sense of the importance of the middle class to the course of a revolution.

Having become conscious of the reality of injustice through the theology and experience of the church in the third world, I was led back to ask what that meant here — in a middle-class church in the middle age of a middle power.

I would like to probe this question in a suggestive, rather than a systematic, fashion. It's not that a systematic approach is unimportant. It is important, and some people must ask in a systematic way: what is the middle class anyway?

Sociologists are now telling us that the middle class is not easily identifiable and that the whole notion of "class" is rapidly shifting as we change from an industrial to an information-based economy. Indeed, some feminists are telling us that "class" is an outmoded category.

Be that as it may, it may still be possible to describe what has become somewhat difficult to define. Middle-class is: some, but not too many kids; mortgages; moving ahead to a point; getting ahead but feeling as though you're falling behind; working more to have more for the less time that is left over; ups and downs.

This middle class could be a liability in the building of an authentic church, or one of its greatest untapped resources. However, the gifts which middle-class people have to bring will never flourish, in the church or in our culture, until these people have experienced the liberation of the gospel of Jesus. Yet the middle class may not hear the gospel of liberation until it knows that it is living in captivity. Unless the middle class recognizes its own captivity, it will never recognize the liberation of the poor as its own liberation.

The most profound form of captivity is the captivity we are not even aware of. And the middle class in North America does not know that it is held captive by the invisible chains of our consumer culture. In one sense, we live in a free country—we do not live behind an iron curtain or a bamboo curtain. But we do live behind a plastic curtain.

What is life like behind the plastic curtain? It is a life held in bondage by many things. Our consumer culture is based on a fundamental perversion: it is a culture in which things have become more important than people. (The neutron bomb, which destroys people but leaves things intact, is the epitome of this culture.) We do not possess things so much as they possess us.

Jesuit philosopher John Kavanaugh has given an incisive analysis of the consumer culture through an examination of advertising. He points out how advertising bombards us with the message that things are more important than people.

Think of these ads: "Don't thank me, thank Listerine." "Coke is the real thing." "Datsun saves and sets you free." In the scriptures, this is called idolatry, worshipping the things we have made.

Notice how the things in these ads seem to take on a personality. In fact, they begin to seem more interesting and attractive than most of the people we know! Notice the people in many of these ads, especially the women. They look so metallic and inhumanly perfect. Functional. They are mechanical dolls who have been wound up to sell things.

In our consumer culture, the middle class learns that marketability is the most important goal. Very early on, every child learns that he or she has a potential market value: love is earned and competed for in the family, education is valued in terms of production and competitive standards, the person who enters the job market must learn to sell himself or herself. Thus, diplomas, skills, talents, and style become the means of increasing one's marketability.

To save ourselves from being shelved, we start to live our human relationships according to the laws of the marketplace – in terms of conflict and competition. We learn the techniques of manipulation, control, and domination. Personal relationships become as disposable as paper cups. In other words: we treat others as we ourselves are being treated – like things.

Why do we keep on doing this? Because we need many things. Our culture tells us (indeed creates within us) the need to consume many things. And so we produce and produce and we ourselves are consumed in the process. Anxious, driven, stressed.

There is little room for joy on the open market – at least, not as a state of being. It does exist, however, as a detergent, and you can buy it just about anywhere. For just a little more money you can get "more joy", "new and improved joy".

Think about the ideal of human living presented in advertising – an ideal often deliberately pitched to the middle class. There we see the impossible dream of someone who looks good, looks great all the time, every minute of the day and night.

Perhaps there are people like this but I have never met them. Imagine the frustration of ordinary middle-class people who believe this propaganda about the model of being human: they can only feel less than perfect most of the time — not rich enough, not beautiful enough, not anything enough. But they keep on trying.

People who live behind a plastic curtain are enslaved by the idea that how they look, what they do, and what they have are more important than who they are. And thus it becomes very difficult for them to experience the liberation of love which the gospel promises.

Those caught in a consumer culture are trained to love others for a reason — for how they look, what they do, what they have. And they expect that they themselves will only be loved for some such reason.

However, the message of Jesus, and of all the scriptures, is that God loves human beings without reasons — loves them just because they are — and because God loves them, they are.

Our culture gives us many reasons for loving many things, for loving people as things. It has little to say about the mystery of the human person, who loves and is loved without reason.

To be a follower of Jesus in this consumer culture means saying, as Pope John Paul has done so eloquently, that the human person has a transcendent value, that the human person is more important than any thing or any system. Yet such a discipleship is difficult because the consumer culture holds us in bondage in so many ways: in our flight from self, in our isolation from others, in patterns of consumptive living, and in broad structural patterns of injustice.

However, there are signs that liberation from our culture is at least desired. A 1981 poll released by Jankelovich indicated that 70 per cent of Americans wanted a less materialistic, a more humane, a more personal way of life. That is a startling and hopeful statistic. Many people know what happiness would mean. The only problem is that they don't know what to do to make that possible.

The church could become the agent of liberation for the middle class in this culture, but it can do so only if it itself becomes a more profoundly spiritual church which values the human person.

This is no easy task because the church itself often shares in the captivity of the middle class. Think how the church tries to sell religion, how it estimates its success in terms of numbers of people who attend liturgies, how liturgies are evaluated. Someone asks, "Was it a good liturgy?" i.e. "Was it a good show?"

One has the impression that the church values only those who are religiously productive. The head offices of some of our churches resemble corporate boardrooms and some retreat houses seem like supermarkets where one can purchase the latest fads in spirituality.

Yet there are signs that some are breaking the bonds of captivity. There are middle-class people who are trying to claim some "useless" time with family and friends, time with nature, time which has no market value. There are people who are taking time to pray, that most "useless" activity where one meets God as a person, where one become more human. Some may denigrate all of this as personalistic spirituality. It is much more than that. In this culture, time spent with people and with God is a form of radical political resistance.

There are signs, too, that the church is becoming more of a community that values human people.

It is a hopeful sign that some Christians are working to bring about social change, change in the structures of our society that hold people in bondage to things. Some Christians are beginning to see how the structures of our society are consuming the unemployed, women, and the handicapped.

It is an even more hopeful sign that some Christians are realizing that these same structures are not only consuming North Americans; they are also consuming people elsewhere, in the third world, and dehumanizing them in a far more obvious and brutal way. Here, the bondage of the consumer culture is experienced through symptoms of stress, anxiety, addictions, and broken personal relationships. There, this bondage is experienced as poverty, famine, torture, and death.

The poor in our society already know in their gut that something is wrong. But many middle-class people are still living in the illusion that this is the best of all possible worlds. They are held captive by many things. They are kept in a state of perpetual motion, never stopping to engage in the dangerous activity of thinking about the illusions that govern their lives. So many middle-class people are captivated by the politics of personal relationships (by the endless wars and negotiations and truces of divorces and affairs) that they do not have the energy to engage in the politics of social change. Those who are captivated by the soap opera of everyday life will hardly see the dirty reality of the society we live in.

To such as these the gospel of liberation must be preached. Let the middle class cast off their invisible chains. Let the poor break their very obvious chains. And let them hold hands together.

## RESTORING THE CHURCH?
(Editorial, CNT, June 17, 1984)

An increasing number of signs indicate that the Vatican is now engaged in a process of "restoring" the church. In Europe and Latin America, progressive theologians have been censured and national conferences of bishops have been reminded of the loyalty which is owed to Rome.

Over the past year, the long arm of the Vatican has

reached out to the North American church. In the United States in particular, there has been a series of what can only be called investigations — of local bishops, of seminaries, of religious communities. Sisters and priests holding public office have been forced to choose between the religious vocation they are living and the religious vocation as it is legislated by Rome. Most recently, the Vatican has placed a publication ban on a book which had the approval of a local bishop in the United States.

There are some North American Catholics of a conservative bent who will welcome such restorative efforts with a sense of rejoicing and perhaps even vindication. However, there are other Catholics, those who greeted Vatican II and its call to renew the church, who will view this attempt at restoration with a sense of fear and foreboding.

This is the time for neither fear nor rejoicing. This is the time to make some sober assessments of the restoration efforts to re-establish the order and uniformity of the pre-Vatican II church of the nineteenth century.

It should come as no surprise that there is a certain desire for such order in the church twenty years after the intensely creative moment of the spirit which was Vatican II. We are now living in an in-between time, in the time between the collapse of the old order and the birth of a new order in the church. This gap between the past and future is as filled with peril as it is with promise.

There is an understandable desire on the part of many conservatives to restore to the church the sense of clarity and cohesion which marked it before Vatican II. The need for some rock of stability in a world of flux and change is not unreasonable. These conservatives experience the pilgrim church of Vatican II as a wandering and indeed drifting church. They are tempted by the illusion that Christendom can be restored by the force of authority.

However, the so-called liberals of this in-between time

are tempted by another illusion, the illusion that they have already arrived at a new form of church. New theologies and programs of church renewal are baptized even before they have come fully to birth. There seems little sensitivity to the need for depth, discipline, and direction in the church if the creative moment of Vatican II is not to dissipate into sheer chaos and confusion.

At this point in the life of the church the illusions guiding the efforts at restoration seem to be gaining in legitimacy. This too is understandable, given the world-wide conservative trends in social and economic life.

Will this effort to restore Christendom continue? With the wisdom of Gamaliel we say: "If it is of God it will survive."

Our estimation is that these restorative measures will not survive because they are measures guided more by the spirit of the world than by the spirit of God. It is ironic, and even tragic, that the goal of protecting the church from the liberal spirit of the world is being implemented through means which are very much of this world — secrecy, backroom politics, the raw use of power and coercive authority. This is all very far from the ways of God and because of this, we believe, the present efforts at restoration will not survive.

Yet will the progressives in the church be able to survive this restoration time until it inevitably fails? Not without a great deal of purification. If the effort to restore the church will not endure because of its coercive methods, the effort to renew the church will endure only because of its attractive elements.

In the end, the renewal of Christianity will not attract long-haul commitment because of new theologies or razzle-dazzle liturgies or relevant programs or critical issues. Only the witness of suffering love, of faithful hope, of persistent prayer, of joyful justice, will attract people

to a church which will live forward into the future because
it stretches far back — beyond the nineteenth century — to
the origins of our Christian tradition.

*July 1984*
So I am sitting up here by this northern lake with all these
books about the Pope and the church and Canada. Surely
there are better things to do with one's summer! But CBC
called me in June to do the commentary for the upcoming
papal visit. My initial response was "Good God, no!" I
knew the visit to the States was a disaster and I didn't
want to be caught between offering incense to the Pope
and paying homage to the Catholic liberal elite. Then
there were more phone calls. "Highly placed sources"
saying, "if you don't do it, imagine who will." The CBC
saying, "There's no one else who would be credible." And
then the grapevine news that the Toronto chancery office
had written Rome saying I was not a credible spokesperson for the Roman Catholic Church. (They may be right!)

So I took all this in. What endured was an imperative
memory — do not abandon responsibility for public life.
And so I have waded in. In between readings I swim in
the deep cool waters and splash around with only the
loons in sight. The loons call hauntingly in the evening.
And I pray for such an echo in my soul, such a clear and
simple echo.

*September 1984*
We are in Vancouver on the last leg of the papal visit to
Canada. Yes, I say "we", because somehow this motley
crew of CBC-TV professionals and we on-the-spot Catholics have become a team of sorts. We all embarked on this
papal tour as a job that we wanted to do well and so we
have.

But we have all been taken aback by the goodness of

this man John Paul II. The executive producer said, "I've been with a thousand politicians and I know a phony when I see one. He isn't a phony."

And it's true. He isn't a phony. I don't agree with everything he says but I now know he believes what he's saying. The goodness and integrity are undeniable. He's not trendy—just truthful in his own way.

And so we have all been caught up in a ten-day journey that we could never have imagined. My cohorts, Peter Mansbridge and Larry Stout, have surprised and delighted me with their openness to what none of us could have scripted. From city to city, from booth to booth, we have watched the soul of our country unfurl before us.

By the time we reached Edmonton, many of us on the CBC team were almost voiceless with various kinds of infections. But we looked out for each other. The goodness was infectious too. If there is one thing I have learned out of this tour, it is that we have a deep and pure longing to see that goodness is real.

Difficult was the stop the Pope made to the church Stephen Roman constructed in Unionville, Ontario. CBC was willing to let it go without comment. But I knew about Roman's influence and I knew he had just made a significant contribution to an educational institution in Poland. I told the executive producer that I had to say something about the apparent inconsistency between the Pope's statements on behalf of the poor and the weight wealth had carried in ensuring the Pope's visit to the church in Unionville. So I said what I thought over TV while Arnold Amber (the producer) was yelling in my ear, "Watch the libel!"

More difficult was the scene at the cathedral in Edmonton, when the Pope acclaimed "the light of Christ" in front of an interfaith group where there were many Jews and Moslems present. Obviously somebody fluffed in the arrangements, and that is a story that remains to be told. But in the moment I was caught on national TV explaining the view of the second Vatican council, which was obviously counter to what the Pope had said and participated in.

And difficult was the encounter with Lois Wilson (the moderator of the United Church) outside the ecumenical service at St. Paul's Anglican Church in Toronto. She was angry. "It's just a show of power." I felt dismissed as one of the papal minions.

I saw the truth of all this but could not deny the goodness.

LIFE AFTER POPE JOHN PAUL II
(CNT, Oct. 14, 1984)

Like a long-distance runner finishing the race, the Canadian church stands still—catching its breath, wondering what happened during those twelve days in September when Pope John Paul outdistanced all expectations.

The critics were confounded by what happened. They asked if thousands of people had taken leave of their senses, had forgotten the latest statistics about the irrelevance of institutional religion, had ignored the recent revelations of Vatican conspiracies.

I watched those thousands of people across Canada from my perch in the CBC-TV anchor booth. These people had not forgotten their questions or their own personal contradictions but they had remembered something more—the need for an altar in their lives, the need to celebrate the mysterious reality of life.

In every major city in this country, the papal visit became the occasion for building an altar, for creating a focal point of reverence and worship. The altars were built in spaces which had been used for picnics, for sports events, and for military purposes. For twelve days, religion moved out of the sanctuaries and permeated the public life of this country.

Around these altars, the church community gathered to celebrate the faith — not as a separate reality but as the ultimate dimensions of all aspects of life.

The critics may have missed the meaning of these altars because they were more aware of the idols, the ideologies which were attendant on the papal visit. Some felt his progressive social statements were masking a more reactionary view of the church. Others tried to ferret out the moles who had tricked the unwitting Pope into making such strong social statements. Political pundits worried about the state of a nation in which people were more willing to follow the Pope than their democratically elected leaders.

On these and other points, the critics and the pundits are not without some insight into the ambiguities of the papal visit. Indeed, they have probably signalled some of the issues which will be with us for some time.

However, those who focus only on the levels of ambiguity in the papal visit may miss that mysterious level, in the church and in the human person, which was touched by John Paul II.

He called forth goodness. It was the desire to touch goodness, in ourselves and in others, that moved thousands of Canadians to stand in the rain and to wait in the cold.

There was a graciousness to his goodness — a quality not easily manufactured. I was confirmed in this perception by the media people who were following the Pope across the country. They are experts in nosing out the difference between the genuine and the glad-handing, between the person and the package. Few agree with all of John Paul's ideas but few would deny that he is a good man.

One rather jaded European correspondent told me that he had been on many papal tours and had seen it all. "But my eyes still filled up when I saw him with those handicapped people."

The goodness rang true even as the discordant notes were sounding. While the pope preached the dignity and value of the human person, the dignity of other religions was being ignored as the so-called interfaith services and women were symbolically undervalued in liturgies. While the Pope defended human rights and the poor, Brazilian theologian Leonardo Boff was being attacked in the Vatican with little respect for due process.

The note of true goodness in John Paul made these discordant notes all the more audible.

The visit of the Pope has become a promise and a judgement for the Canadian church. There is hope in the fact that so many desire to worship, desire to touch goodness — even in a culture that creates the continual need for canned goods. It would seem that the time is ripe for faith. Yet the exceptional response to John Paul serves to prove the rule that the institutional church has not been tapping into the wellsprings of the spirit which still run deep below the surface of Western culture.

Canadian Catholics could try to live off the papal visit — for a while. We could develop programs to extend and deepen the understanding of what he was saying during his visit here. It would be interesting and inviting — for a while. But it was the person of John Paul who breathed life and spirit into his speeches. It was the graciousness of goodness which touched so many — and that quality cannot be programmed, packaged, or sold. It can only be lived, practised, prayed for.

*New Year's Day, 1985*
There was lots of talk at the gathering, but nothing sticks in my mind today. I think Mark gave a ferverino about fidelity being more important than success. My overwhelming need is to be silent, to be alone. I've been so very busy (still trying to get someone to replace me at CNT) but I'm not sure where I am in it all. That's why I know I need to go away on this thirty-day retreat in January. I need to stop and pray, to make some choices for the future.

I spent a lot of time last night doing dishes in the kitchen. I think my friends realize the retreat will be an important time for me. One by one they came into the kitchen and said they'd be praying for me. Sometimes the best thing we can do for each other is to send each other to our solitude.

# IV

*A Modicum of Light*

*January 1985 (Our Lady of Peace Spiritual Life Center, Narragansett, Rhode Island)*
I feel like a sputtering old car that has barely made it to the gas station. But I have made it here, and there's no place else in the world that I would rather be at this moment. When I first met Sister Kieran Flynn (who's supposed to accompany me on this retreat) I thought I was meeting some wise old Irish relative. There's something about her eyes — sparkling, laughing, far-seeing. I thought she'd be fun to talk with. Right and oh so wrong.

In our first conversation I wanted to tell her all about myself and what I was doing; my questions and concerns were all lined up. She didn't seem that impressed, and in five minutes gently knocked away all my usual props. "You're bored to death, deeply bored. You don't know who you are. You are an infinite hunger and thirst for God. If you don't live out of that truth you're going to burn up from frustration, and you'll burn everyone else around you."

It's true. Underneath all the activity and excitement there's something in me that isn't quite alive. Not quite alive to God?

But Kieran seems alive, more than alive. She told me that she was dying of multiple melanoma a few years ago and had been given three weeks to live. Some friends asked her if they could pray for her healing. "That was the most difficult decision. The pain was so awful I wanted to die. But somehow I said yes to their prayers. Three days later there was no sign of cancer. That's the ultimate freedom — to be free to die or free to live." It's as if she sees things from the other side. And I think that's why she feels so free and clear about rattling my cage — she doesn't need me to like her (which I do, enormously); she wants me to be free.

And she says, "Be attentive to your dreams." I've been so attentive to the world around me ("reality") that I wonder if I dream any more. "Do not belittle your dreams."

Mostly I spend my days walking along the deserted beaches of this summer resort town — or sitting in a crevice in the rocks with my thermos of coffee and my copy of the scriptures. Somehow the waves are pulling me into a deeper wash of time....

Recalling a conversation with Kieran about a talented friend of hers who had helped a great many people and was now dying: "She gave so much to them — time, energy, all her talent. She gave everything but herself." She could be me....

Out on the rocks today I felt I could hardly breathe. Gasping for air. At that moment, I felt I was like Christopher in his incubator, gasping for air. Felt I *was* Christopher. I was just this someone who couldn't do anything, who was so weak and frail. And yet. And yet, I felt I was known by name and loved, just as we had known and loved

Christopher. Heard God saying: "You don't have to do anything." Stayed there on the rocks for hours. When I returned, all the anxious strivings and provings had fallen away.

Little Christopher has returned as the deepest truth of myself. All he was, all I am, is love. Without reason, now and for ever. Amen.

Kieran asked me to write out the things in my life that call for sorrow, for forgiveness. The sorrow is that so much of my life has been spent in constructing my "self". In spite of all the religious rhetoric, I have become a self-made person. I have not trusted, in myself or others, the mystery that life is a gift that I could never have manufactured on my own. While I don't have many possessions (like those whom I criticize so readily and so publicly), I have treated my very self as a possession. And I have protected this possession, from God and from others. As though I sit on the rock that is me and refuse to trust myself to the waves. Sure, I get involved in things, but it's all on the shoreline. And out there, in here, is something infinitely mysterious.

So let me stop thinking about "I" and let me say, "Yes, You are the God of my life, You are my life."

Let me choose between the self I have made and the self that is being created by You....

I've written out on pieces of paper the aspects of my self that I have created or that others have. The partly true, and therefore false, identities. There's lots of pieces of paper! One by one I've burned them. The last two pieces of paper, the last identities I could let go of, were my sense of humour and my talent for writing. But I let them go and knew I was still there, as Christopher was. And I scattered the ashes into the waves.

I cannot save myself. I cannot be myself. I cannot save anyone else. The self I make will become false. The self

others make of me will become false. I cannot unmake
myself or anyone else. Without You, God, everything good
about myself will ultimately undo me and others....

So maybe for the first time (no, it can't be the first) I
understand who Jesus was, is. The one whose life was
given, not taken away....

This last morning at Narragansett, I walked once more
along the shore early in the morning. All so still. Like
being at peace. Like the first morning of the resurrection.
No trumpets, orchestras, or parades. Just a still being.

Resolution: I must make some moves towards pulling
back from *Catholic New Times* and the *Toronto Star* commitment. It's a choice to spend less time reacting to "as
it happens" and more time responding to what is.

### RETREAT TO THE TRUTH
(TS, Feb. 23, 1985)

I write this column in utter stillness—from the place by
the ocean where I have been "on retreat" for the past
month.

There are those who will feel uncomfortable at the
thought of someone being "on retreat". It suggests a flight,
an admission of defeat. Yet "making a retreat" is a long-
honoured practice in the Christian tradition. Paradoxically, the time of retreat was the time of confrontation. In
the first centuries of Christianity, God-driven people
made their way out into the desert not to escape but to
wrestle with the demons. The desert was the place for the
searing search for truth.

Now, as then, it is not easy to seek a place of interior
truth. To leave behind illusions about oneself, others, the
church, and society is to risk the mirages of the mind. One

needs a guide and well-springs within to take the desert route. Then begins the process of abandoning the baggage which lugs us around in our journey through life.

Leave behind the chatter—and what can we say?

Leave behind the job—and is there anything left to do?

Leave behind our daily routine—and how do we function?

Leave behind pressure—and what is left to get us going?

Leave behind TV—and what images cross our flickering minds?

Leave behind our social classification—and is there anything left to define us?

Leave behind the people of our lives—and is there anyone there?

What remains?

Perhaps only the still small sense that we are more than what we do, what we own, where we live, and who others say we are.

Who are we in truth? In the desert space we sense simply that we are—of God, with God, for God. As in the beginning. And it is very good.

Only when we have found ourselves in the heart of goodness can the questions worth asking begin to shape our lives. "To whom shall we go? Where do you live? Who do you say I am?" These are the questions born somewhere between the marrow and the bone.

Questions of the heart are not easily answered but they can, none the less, be lived with and responded to. Without these questions, our lives shrivel on the surface and narrow into nothingness. We ask these questions only because God is already in quest of us. We respond to these questions with bone endings, leaps of nerve. Our response to these questions will determine with whom we cast our lot, where we draw the line, how we count our blessings.

THE POINT OF POWER
(TS, March 23, 1985)

Any fly on the wall will tell you that the real agenda of many a women's meeting is power. It is a topic that not a few chairmen would like to rule out of order.

My own opinion is that power is indeed the point for women, but that this point will be disappointing if it is not pursued to the end.

Women began to pursue power when consciousness dawned, when they were sick and tired of being sick and tired. To get out from under, we wanted power over. Once we knew we were employees of just about everybody, we began to dream of being president of the corporation. It seemed like liberation but it bound us even more closely to the form of power which has been culturally experienced as male. We became like that which we were fighting against. We bought the definition of power as possession — a thing which some possessed and many did not, a thing which some had a lot of and many had a little of. We bought the definition of power as private property. Power was a possession for which one sold oneself. It was a possession worth fighting for, worth dying for. It was not a peaceable form of power.

Women who won such power feared its loss and yet felt guilty about possessing it. Such power, some of us are learning, enslaves the haves as well as the have nots. Those who possess such power become possessed by it.

This kind of power is so seductive that some religious people have preferred the relative purity of weakness and powerlessness. Some of our finest spiritual masters have provided us with religious reasons for preferring weakness to such oppressive strength. Yet, beyond the dawning and dimming of women's consciousness, there is a growing sense of another kind of power which is more appropriate for women and, ultimately, more appropriate for humanity.

We are beginning to have a sense that power is not "power over" but "power with". Power is not an object, not a pie to be possessed or divided so that a larger share for some means a smaller share for others. As the philosopher Hannah Arendt has written, power is the energy generated when people come together. We begin to act when we interact.

We do not possess such power, nor does it possess us; such power liberates all. This is the kind of power which is the stronger for being shared. This power creates equals and allies, not opponents and enemies. It is the kind of power worth living with, worth living for. The dream becomes not that of being president of the corporation but of changing the corporation so that there are no more presidents!

There are moments, like a recent day sponsored by Toronto Women of Faith, when such a dream seems real. Yet how easily the dream grows dim. If we face the less than human reality of our time (massive starvation, organized injustice, the nuclear arms race) we are forced to admit that even a new form of human power is — only human.

Perhaps, at this point, we may admit our need for a more than human power. Such power is beyond, not outside of, ourselves. To draw on such power we must draw near to the mysterious centre of our lives where we are who we really are. This mystery is the point of our lives — beyond us, encompassing us, and nearer to us than we are to ourselves.

From this mysterious centre, we experience our limitless solidarity with every human being. At this centre, we know that we are neither victims nor masters. At this still point, we know ourselves as an infinite desire for freedom and love. This is the point of our power.

BETWEEN EMMAUS AND JERUSALEM
(CNT, April 7, 1985)

My generation grew up in the Galilee of the sixties, in all the big and little secular cities of our growing wild and greening. Our Nazareth was football and Saturday night and music which was more than melody. Our Nazareth was also First Fridays, Lenten resolutions, and visits to the crib. Something good can come out of all that. We were frivolous and fervent and fabulously generous. We wanted to walk on water — like Kennedy, like Tom Dooley.

We could afford to fish around for something to do with our lives. While we were casting around and testing the winds, we heard a call from a round old man who walked in the shoes of the fisherman. Pope John XXIII was our breath of fresh air. We hoisted our sails and caught the winds of change in the church. The hope of Vatican II became our hope and we became disciples of renewal in the church. It was a time for visions and we had been born to dream. We were the war babies — first signs of life in a burnt-out world. We were booming, the church was booming — and busting.

Pope John died, Dooley died, the Kennedys and King were killed. Many of our teachers, prophets, and priests left the church. We were a generation left without idols. We were ready to begin our public ministry.

From pulpits, and in workshops and demonstrations, we began to preach the good news of renewal. We hoped for community, participation, justice, and love. We worked hard, planned hard, and prayed hard. We believed that on the edge of today was the tomorrow when our hope would be realized. Through the sixties and seventies we pushed towards Jerusalem — the city of our high hope.

Twenty years after Vatican II, we came to Jerusalem — but we never arrived at the city of our dreams. We came to a pile of stones where the high priests of Rome and the governors of imperial powers began to put our hopes on trial. Laws were invoked to nail down our hopes and we began to doubt they had ever existed.

We invested a lot in the renewal of our church — money, time, and energy. And it didn't seem to be paying off. We had not learned to live with failure, frustration, and fear. We underestimated the powers that be, the fear of change, and the weight of history. Blinded by righteousness and deaf to legitimate criticism, we overestimated our own virtue. We were oblivious of the high priest and governor within ourselves.

Soul Doubt.

We began to feel overpowered by reactionary forces in the church. As long as we could criticize those who were burying our hopes, we could deny our own betrayals of the gospel. In the gathering darkness, we could avoid our own shadows. We legitimized our obsessions, excused our secret deals with fear, and pursued petty forms of protection. We forgot all those stories about mustard seeds, withered vines, and ungrateful servants.

We conducted private burials for our hope. We walked away from Jerusalem so slowly that we did not even know we were leaving. We walked away from the city of our buried hope, dawdling along with companions. We turned towards Emmaus, the small place where we could domesticate our hopes, where we could surround ourselves with survivors, where we could set up shop and display our spiritual wares. In Emmaus, we could cultivate a garden of giving up. Jerusalem could be left to the high priests and governors.

But He whom we had followed to Jerusalem was now following us as we made our way to Emmaus. We told Him of our broken hopes and the fears we would bury in Emmaus. He began to retell the story we had almost forgotten. It was a story of hope — not the story of our hope but the story of God's hope in us.

We recognized Him as He broke the bread of the hope that He had been throughout all our other hopes. We understood then that our deepest hope would not be buried for ever.

So we stand here on the road — knowing that one way leads to Emmaus, to a grinding halt, and the other way leads to Jerusalem — where we will not rest in peace.

*May 1985*
Still astounded by the revelation during the visit home in Saskatoon: Dad decided to go up to the attic and get down his old war diary. He hasn't had time to do this until now. I asked him if I could read it — wanting to and yet not wanting to. Caught between wanting to keep him as my father and wanting to know him before he was my father. The diary has been a revelation. It's clear from the entries that I was conceived around VE Day. Dad was on leave from the Continent for a few days and barely made it back to England to see Mom. I kept thinking, "What if he had missed the boat?!" The shock of realizing that I could just as easily have not been born. And once again this primal wave of gratitude. This is the most amazing grace — to have been given a chance to live. And once again this sense of an unearned gift, an unseen light that seems to encircle all the darkness that follows.

Is it possible that my concern for peace began on the first day of peace in Europe? This is all beyond me.

*September 1985*

The long-promised letter from Basya Hunter arrived today. I must admit I awaited it and dreaded it. She had called me in June at the office and wanted to have lunch. Wouldn't take no for an answer. I remembered her as the author of the play *Johannes Reuchlin and the Talmud.* I suspected she wanted to talk about Jewish-Christian relations. But no – she wanted to talk about my writing. Said she had been clipping things from the *Toronto Star* and had been to several of my talks. She wanted to know why I thought of myself as a journalist. She demanded to see samples of my writing. I couldn't dismiss her – any more than I could have dismissed the challenge Kieran had presented to me.

Basya had told me her own story: her family, of Russian Jewish background, had settled in New York. She was interested in drama and sailed back to Moscow to study theatre in the days when Russia was still within the Western pale. On the boat she met Peter Hunter, a young Canadian fired with socialist dreams who wanted to study Marxism. They married and returned to Toronto to the struggles of the cold war, to their own disillusionment with Stalinism, and to years of criticism from the Jewish community and the Canadian public, who viewed the Communist Party with suspicion. One of their friends was Emil Fackenheim, the young rabbi at Holy Blossom Temple who had escaped from Germany. I remembered meeting Basya and Peter at a Passover meal at the Fackenheims'. She had become a teacher at a Hebrew school and then began producing and writing her own plays.

In her long shawl, lashes, and semi-theatrical wardrobe, I didn't know if she was an angel or a temptress as we sat over lunch.

And now the letter. "Almost immediately during my first hurried reading, I knew that you have to write, that your need to write will be with you forever no matter what price you will have to pay for it. The need will cry out and deafen you in the insatiable longing to have your heart and your word beat together. The need I am talking about is not the one which grows exclusively out of ideological responsibility to teach and to clarify. The need I mean is the mystery in the human being whose essence is like the plant that turns towards the sun."

An angel with a message.

*November 1985*
I'm here in Baltimore for a gathering of representatives of religious congregations from Canada, the United States, and Latin America (The Fifth Interamerican Meeting). The concerns seem so urgent and the commitment so real. Hovering in the background is Archbishop Fajolio — a representative of the Vatican. Supposedly he is here to monitor all the dangerous activity. But he doesn't really understand English or Spanish. We are trying to be courteous and kind, to make him feel welcome.

Last night he announced he was throwing a social evening to which we were all invited. We thought, isn't that nice. We arrived to find that he had ordered in Italian wine and pizza. Isn't that nice, we thought. Then, in the middle of the gathering, he announced through a translator that he had such a big admiration for all the women here that he wanted to sing a song for them. The cassette blared out a tape from an Italian opera and he began to sing along with profound feeling, hands crossed over his chest. The song was "Mama", to his mother.

A Fellini movie. Here he was warbling his heartfelt song to his mother and meanwhile the American women (and the rest of us) were in a state of apoplexy. Some turned white, some almost swallowed their wine glasses. One guy slumped in his chair saying, "Oh Jesus!"

We're worried about priests and sisters being tortured in Latin America and he's singing songs to his mother! Yes, a Fellini movie.

*New Year's Day, 1986*
My contribution to the festivities was a rendition of Fajolio's paean of praise to "Mama". I brought a tape of the song and delivered it with all the roly-poly religiosity I could.

At least we could laugh at this Vatican type. It's more difficult to poke fun at the foibles of the left. Some of them really think they are infallible. Isabel told us how she had been trashed by some feminists at a college symposium. She's still really hurting and angry at their claim to define what is "orthodox" feminism. I have been bothered by discreet phone calls from some in the Catholic left—upset because we hadn't reported on something the way they thought we should, i.e. we included some uncomfortable facts. They appreciate me as a mouthpiece until I speak my mind.

Jim said: "Beware of the granola heads!"

I told the others that there was some (remote) possibility of my being elected to a leadership position in my community. It would mean living in Rome, travelling a lot, and working in a variety of languages.

As I was thinking out loud, several things surfaced. One of the most difficult aspects of such a move would be that of leaving my language and culture. That I would miss my family and friends goes without saying. But who would I be if I couldn't express myself in my own language? It's not just the words, it's that the words are a way of thinking, of feeling, of breathing.

I sense myself walking between two old women, each holding out an arm to show a way—Basya and Kieran. One says I must write to become who I am; the other says

I will not be free to write until I am free not to write—
until I know that my identity is far more than that of being
a writer.

As I walk along with them, I feel more drawn to the
path Kieran is pointing to. Somehow, I want to believe
that even in another language, even if I never wrote
another thing, something of me would still be true, still
be loving.

Ann thought this was altogether too spiritual. "Just
remember there are a lot of people like Fajolio in Rome—
and worse!"

I sense that the new depth of life that opened up for
me on the retreat has made it somewhat more difficult for
me to express myself—the words don't come as quickly or
easily. There seems less to say and what I want to say is
really something quite simple.

### ONE DOES WHAT ONE CAN
(TS, March 22, 1986)

Beautiful Catherine Deneuve looked out from the TV set
and said, in all her languid seriousness, "You can't change
the world but you can change your moisturizer." Alarm
bells started ringing in my head. Has it come to this?

It is coming to this. Read the various Gallup polls which
are published regularly in the *Toronto Star* and see all the
indications of people who feel they can't change the world.
So many are anxious about the future, afraid of global war,
worried about the economy, and dubious about political
leaders—especially Brian Mulroney (the chin in search of
a man).

The sense of powerlessness is pervasive. People feel
unable to change the course of events which is carrying
them along willy-nilly.

Thus begins the retreat into the private and personal world – the only world that seems, at first sight, within our capacity to change. Some throw themselves energetically into working out and working through their personal relationships. But, as in the soaps, the interpersonal world balloons to cosmic proportions. Each encounter with another becomes a point of struggle between the forces of life and the forces of darkness. Others journey within in an effort to change the inner world. Yet the inner world soon reveals itself as as vast, as complex and mysterious, as the world without. In our efforts to change ourselves or our relationships with others, we often feel as helpless as in our attempts to change the world.

And so there remains the possibility of changing our moisturizer, our gum, our eyelashes, our aftershave, or our hair colour. All of these changes help us put a face on things. For the powerless, change is always cosmetic.

Is there any alternative to this cosmic sense of powerlessness and the cosmetic way of life it engenders? My sense is that there is a way through, and beyond, this cover-up – if we learn something about humility. This traditional Christian virtue is much more than a pious practice. In these times, it has great political significance – if it is practised authentically.

Saint Thomas Aquinas described humility as the habit of acting beyond the two extremes of false pride and false humility. False pride might be, for example, the illusion that we must do everything to change the world, while false humility would be the illusion that we can do nothing to change the world. Both of these attitudes leave us with a sense of powerlessness. The one leads to burn-out and the other to rust-out.

Authentic humility says, "I cannot do everything to change the world but I can do something." Each of us must discover what that "something" is.

Authentic humility is well illustrated in the story of the rabbit and the little chick who were walking along the road when the sky began to fall. The rabbit ran as fast as he could and then noticed that the little chick had not followed. The rabbit shouted back, "Little chick, little chick, the sky is falling." But the little chick didn't move. The rabbit raced back and saw the little chick lying on his back, legs in the air, toes spread wide. "Little chick, what are you doing?" asked the rabbit. "One does what one can," replied the little chick as he stretched his toes wider.

### GREGORY BAUM: CONSCIOUSLY AND CONSISTENTLY CHOOSING TO AFFIRM THE LIGHT
### (CNT, May 4, 1986)

Zena Cherry, who reports on high society events for the *Globe and Mail*, has not been invited to the evening of appreciation for Gregory Baum on May 6. Pity. It would be fun to see her try to describe the people who will be present that evening. They are not people who would fit comfortably into her usual categories, which are meant to cover the executives of whatever who attend whatever "with their wives".

Those who come to express their gratitude for Gregory Baum's time in Toronto will probably attend "with their friends", "with their community", or "with their husbands"! It will be a gathering of people from the many worlds of Gregory Baum.

There are few who live in as many worlds as Gregory and fewer still who do so with such ease and grace. And yet Toronto has been the concrete place he called home for twenty-seven years. Now Gregory is leaving this city for a new position at McGill University in Montreal.

Gregory will be missed in many places in Toronto. He

will be most noticeably absent from his cluttered office at St. Michael's College, where he could be found, typing away, from the early hours of almost every day. This was the place where he produced several important books and hundreds of articles for publications of every sort. No history of Vatican ii will be complete without taking account of what he wrote during his years in Toronto.

Graduate students will miss the man behind the open door of that office. I speak from experience. One morning, having reached that point of despair known only to those writing a dissertation, I knocked on Gregory's door. Half an hour and a cup of coffee later, I was on my way — shored up with some suggestions which made it all seem worthwhile and even possible. This moment of encouragement from Gregory was not exceptional — it was the rule for a whole generation of students at St. Michael's College. And in the classroom, Gregory was an example of how to think without walls, of how to move beyond the institutional or psychological barriers which had kept theology confined and theologians protected from examination by the world beyond the halls of academia.

Gregory's was a portable classroom. He taught in church basements, in noisy labour halls, in stuffy meeting rooms, and in the ramshackle studios of radio stations. Like it or not, people knew what he was talking about. He had imposed upon himself the discipline of simplicity, the difficult task of synthesizing complex issues in a way that enabled more people to discuss those issues.

Gregory will be missed at 80 Sackville St., at the offices of *Catholic New Times*. He has been one of our greatest supporters — contributing financially in times of distress, and creatively, by producing articles at a moment's notice. He was an editor's delight. No one ever had to cater to his ego.

There were times when Gregory dropped by the *Catho-*

*lic New Times* offices simply to say hello, keep up the good work, thanks for everything. As it was with us, so it was with many other small and strictly non-profit groups in the city. He has a way of appreciating the humblest of efforts and he taught us how to value what we were trying to do even when the fruits of our efforts seemed meagre.

Nevertheless, there will be some joy in Muddy York — and relief in the local chancery office — when Gregory Baum departs from the scene. There are some Catholics in the city, and even some faculty members at St. Michael's College, who feel that the Toronto church is well rid of his influence. For these people, Gregory has become a symbol of those who have led the church so far down the garden path that it has become overgrown with the weeds of worldliness. He is a handy scapegoat for those who seem unable to face the self-destructive tendencies in themselves or in the church.

The man who is Gregory Baum is far more constructive than the myths of his destructive power suggest. His critical reflections are not divorced from his desire to create a deeper sense of the human community, of the church community. He is constantly recovering elements of the Christian tradition which can be brought to bear on contemporary life and questions.

In recent years, Gregory has drawn more obviously on Christian practices from the past as resources for the long-haul commitment to justice and peace. An example: a few years ago, he was bed-ridden with a back injury. His enforced stillness became for him an opportunity to practise again the more passive form of meditation he had learned in his novitiate days. He remarked at the time that many activists flounder in times of personal suffering because they have not learned the habit of meditation. "Action," he said, "is always carried by a passive dimension, by a reception of the transcendent gifts of God."

I was constantly impressed, indeed amazed, by Gregory's positive attitude towards the church. He had seen the underside of the church in his thorough study of the anti-Semitic strain in Christian history. He had run up against the corruption of Vatican bureaucrats during his days as a theological expert at Vatican II. He had seen the heavy burdens laid on the backs of lay people by a clergy who had little idea of the realities of married life. As he consciously placed himself in solidarity with various marginalized groups (women, the poor), he became more aware of the abuse of power in the church. He had personally experienced the arrogant use of authority in the church. (The story remains to be told of how he was pushed out of the priesthood, by the powers-that-be in the Canadian church, long before he jumped.)

Yet Gregory refuses to indulge in petulant put-downs of the church. Over the years, he seems to have come to some clear inner feeling which distinguishes him from those who cannot admit that the church has any cracks, and from those who project all of their own flaws onto the church. I have sometimes seen Gregory shake his head on hearing those compulsive defenders or carping critics: "They must both let go of the dream of finding the perfect mother in the church," he has said. He sees this impossible dream leading to dangerous delusions, on the one hand, or bitter disappointment, on the other.

Gregory is not too surprised by the weakness of the church. He continues to be amazed at its surprising goodness. There are those who feel he is almost too positive about the church. They attribute this to an optimistic temperament or even see it as a strategy he has adopted in order to survive relatively unscathed at a time when there seem to be search-and-destroy missions aimed at theologians.

It does seem as if Gregory has been blessed with a

happy outlook on life, an attitude that has enabled him to retain a certain buoyancy in the midst of the traumatic events of his adolescence — his escape as a young Jew from the infernos of Nazi Germany, his stint in an internment camp in Canada. And it is true that being constructive is a good strategy for these times in the church.

However, for Gregory, living constructively is also a conscious act of faith. There are times when I have glimpsed that faith which is fashioned in the darkness. After one heavy meeting, during which many of us were made more aware of the extent of grave injustices everywhere, Gregory mused out loud that, while he had been more optimistic when he was younger, his sense of the darkness in the world seemed to increase as he got older. "In face of this," he said, "we must consciously and consistently choose to affirm the light. We must not add to the darkness."

## July 1986

Just before I left for this meeting in Jerusalem, I told the *Toronto Star* that I couldn't continue the column. It seemed to me as if I was manufacturing words for a deadline, something I had resolved not to do. I want what I write to have more to do with a life-line.

This community gathering in Jerusalem has relieved me of the burden of the job in Rome. The meeting is predictable prose, prosaics easily translatable. I know we all need some poetry, some flash of form that emerges with content. Yet it has not been given to any of us, or to all of us.

Here in Jerusalem we are as overcome by daily realities as any of those struggling to make their living along the way of the cross.

*October 1986*

Notes on two films: strange how some films can cast up the frames of what you already sensed and barely knew.

The opening sequence of *The Decline of the American Empire* (Denys Arcand): a rather jaded academic talks to a young reporter about the current state of affairs. In a time of historical decline, she says, people cease to invest their energy in a common social project and turn towards more individually oriented projects such as personal development and fulfilment of the self. Only in developing societies, she lectures, is there a social vision which is compelling enough to invite individuals to transcend their personal interests for the sake of something greater.

And in those five opening minutes, I understood the dynamic of so many of the issues we have been covering at *Catholic New Times*. They are stories shaped by two different responses to "the decline of the empire". On the one hand, we have the conservatives who are trying to reverse the process of decline by going back to some more secure social order, and on the other hand, the liberals who have retreated into developing the world of the self.

I have always thought of our culture as the developed world. What would it mean (and what a terrifying thought) to think of ourselves as part of a declining culture? And yet, and yet. Perhaps that is the call of this hour – to live the truth of this moment – with honesty *and* hope. There is no time or place that is nearer to or farther from God – as long as one lives one's life in truth.

And then *The Mission*, and another quite different opening sequence. One Jesuit is sent plunging over a waterfall on a crucifix, and another climbs back up the sheer face of rock with his flute – for the sake of a people he has never known or seen, for the sake of the gospel. I found myself crying, sobbing. I wondered: for what, for whom, would I climb up a waterfall? For what, for whom, would I ask anyone else to climb up a waterfall? And I knew I wanted such a reason. I ached for such a reason.


DISCERNING IN THE DARK
(CNT, Dec. 7, 1986)


In the beginning that was *Catholic New Times* we wrote of the future in the first editorial — and never looked back. This was not only inevitable (given the little experience we had to back us up), but also a choice. Ten years ago, we committed ourselves to fostering the signs of hope we saw in our church and in our world. "We believe something new is coming to birth."

It is only appropriate, then, that we celebrate this anniversary of the *Catholic New Times* by looking ahead once more. Ten years to the good, we have a developed experience of intense participation in the life of the church to draw on in discerning the shape of the future.

These years have put us in contact with many people in Canada and elsewhere who are living "the good news" for our times. They have lent light to our lives and a measure of grace to the grimmest of moments. In recent years, their spreading light seems even brighter as we become more aware of the contrasting darkness which surrounds us and, indeed, is within us. The more we have searched out the light of justice, the more we have become aware of the dark realities of the culture we live in, and of how this darkness is overshadowing the church which has nurtured our deepest hopes.

We are beginning to see that, through all of our various articles, we have been reporting on the larger and longer story of the struggle of a church which is living in a culture in a state of decline. That culture is the consumer culture, fashioned in every far-flung reach of the American empire. We, as Canadians, are living in a colony situated on the edge of that declining empire. As Christians we are part of the established religion in this empire, but we remain largely unconscious of the ways in which this declining culture is subtly determining some of the present directions of the church in North America.

It is not easy to see the slow and sliding decline of our culture. It is difficult to see the proverbial nose on our social façade. There is so much that seems upbeat, "new and improving". Our political leaders give us a daily dish of political pablum. They tell us that we live in the best of all possible worlds.

If not the present, then perhaps the past can provide us with some insight into the deteriorating state of our culture. History is full of stories of great empires that rose and fell despite their illusions of being eternal. One such was the Roman empire, which declined and died and threatened to draw the early Christian church into its downward spiral.

Rome did not fall in a day or even in a year. Its decline took place over a period of centuries, slowly but inexorably. As the imperial power which controlled most of the then-known world overreached its political and economic limits, the overarching vision upon which Rome was constructed began to crumble. The famous Roman law, originally designed to secure justice for its citizens, eventually served only to defend privileges for its elite. The resources of its colonies were used to cater to the insatiable appetites of those who ruled the empire. The decline of this empire was characterized by greed, trivial pursuits, sexual decadence, and religious obsessions. In an effort to stop this pattern of decline, the governors of Rome enacted repressive laws that were simultaneously rigid and inconsistent. But a sense of common social vision, once lost, could not be forcibly retrieved through legislation. Without a guiding vision of the future, individuals retreated to the pursuit of their personal goals and pleasures. By the time this cultural decline reached its nadir, Christianity had become the established religion of the empire.

Today, the American empire shows similar signs of decline: the loss of a collective vision and the ensuing preoccupation with individual fulfilment; the coercive use of power to hold the empire together; internal decadence and rigid defensiveness in the face of external threat.

Trivial pursuits: domed stadiums. Star Wars. The decline may be delayed but, if history teaches us anything, it is irreversible. And now it seems that the whole of the Western world is being drawn into the decline of the American empire. The church, which seems so inextricably linked to Western culture, faces the challenge of going with the flow or determining some other direction.

We see several options before the church at this time. In popular terms, we define one option as the "conservative" and the other as the "liberal" option. Conservatives have a sense of loss in the face of the disintegration of Western culture and the absence of the unifying vision of the church. They seek some form of defence against what they see as the demoralizing effects of a culture in chaos. The church conservatives are in touch with the dangers of life in a declining culture, but only selectively so. Their rightful concerns, about the perils of individualism and the addiction to pleasure, have blinded them as to how they themselves have internalized another pattern of the empire — the imperialistic use of power.

Ultimately the conservative option maintains a fatal link between the church and the declining empire. It is the dying illusion of any empire, religious or secular, that a common vision can be constructed through the coercive use of power. We will not save the barque of Peter from the storms of these times by battening down the hatches and throwing the dissidents overboard, but only by lifting the sail to catch the breath of the Spirit.

The liberals are more aware that the unifying visions of the culture or church, which used to animate an authentic unity, can be used to justify rigid uniformity. The liberal concern is to retrieve some sure space for individual freedom, self-fulfilment, and even personal integrity in the face of a collective ideology that exults in unity, the common good, national security, etc. The liberals' suspicion of imposed uniformity quite rightly leads them to espouse human rights in the church, due process, greater pluralism, and respect for individual conscience in areas such as sexual morality. Yet this suspicion renders them more insensitive to the deep human desire for a common vision to live by. Without such a vision, liberalism can easily degenerate into political and economic selfishness, psychological narcissism, religious flippancy, moral dilettantism, and even decadence.

There is a third option. It is the option that emerged for the church in the times of the decline of Rome. It is also the option *Catholic New Times* committed itself to ten years ago. "We see something new happening in the lives of so many people. The strength of this new life breaks through previous definitions and includes the most diverse kinds of people and movements." Now we are even more convinced that this option opens up a way of life for us.

As Rome declined, small new Christian communities began to develop: communities united by the vision of the gospel, communities which, while resisting the myths of the empire, integrated the fragments of all that had been best in Roman culture. Some of these communities eventually became monastic orders which created small units of a truly Christian society.

The memory of these communities calls us, not back to romantic illusions of monasticism, but forward in recognition of the potential exercised today by small communities of faith animated by visions of the gospel—visions which invite a commitment, a sacrifice, and generosity. These communities may be parish groups, action groups, support groups, prayer groups; religious, clerical, or lay.

These small collectivities of hope, in our country and elsewhere, will not deflect the decline of the American empire, but they will serve to determine an alternative. However, it has become clear to us over these ten years that such communities do not easily spring up—nor, once begun, will they automatically continue.

The daily living out of a possible alternative is a difficult option. It calls for a spirituality for which we ourselves are still searching. But even now, we see the outline of such a spirituality in small communities of faith. It will be a spirituality of a community of disciples who have chosen a certain discipline for their lives in order to live out the gospel option for the long haul. Such a disciplined way of life will sustain us in prayer, reflection, and a lifestyle that supports prophetic action.

It will be a spirituality realized in concrete solidarity with those who are being eaten up by the corrosive effects of the declining empire. It will be a spirituality of forgiveness. We humbly recognize that the patterns of the culture, which are within ourselves and others, will lead us to betray the promise of the kingdom. Yet we believe that, as with Peter, this betrayal will not be the last word about us.

It will be a spirituality of small groups that gather in Eucharistic prayer—a sacrament that gathers up the fragments of our lives and our culture in the deeper unity of the spirit of Jesus. The Eucharist is an ambiguous sacrament for many Catholics today because its external form reflects so many patterns of the empire. Yet our belief in the transforming presence of Jesus in the midst of this symbolic ambiguity leads us to believe that Jesus is also present as the source of transforming power even in the midst of our even more ambiguous world.

This spirituality will above all be a spirituality of celebration, of rejoicing in the small signs of the kingdom. And that is why we celebrate these ten years of the life that has been *Catholic New Times*. It is a moment to celebrate this little sign that our future lies not with the empire but with the Kingdom of God.

*New Year's Day, 1987*
Someone brought a tape of the music from *The Mission*. Again, I got all weepy. Tried to explain why: that we no longer have such a greatness of purpose, which can summon up such commitment and generosity; we no longer have a strong sense of shared meaning in our church or in our communities.

One by one, all the others said that they too have similar feelings from time to time:

Ann—"I'm writing all these articles because I have to. I don't know what I'd write if I wasn't trying to get tenure."

Mark—"Sometimes I think it would be easier to be crucified. Now I'm just being stoned to death with popcorn."

Bill—"I run around like crazy all day—hardly knowing what I am doing or why. But late at night I go into Ann's room and look at her sleeping. I just love looking at her. That's when I know the point of it all. And I feel very centred. I know why."

Susan—"And when Bill's finished looking at Ann, I go into her room too. It's my contemplative moment."

Jim—"It's my two boys that get me up in the morning and make me want to keep going. But I don't have anyone with whom I share a sense of common purpose. Everyone's out for himself in my world. I remember the kind of generosity there was when I first went to the seminary. It's a memory like an ache."

Isabel — "I find a lot of meaning in my teaching. Even if the results aren't always obvious, there is a certain satisfaction in seeing some students getting excited about learning. Still, I feel lonely. It's not just being single, it's feeling alone in some of the things I really believe in."

We began to talk about some of the places where we had seen an energetic sense of purpose and meaning. I am resolved to pursue this discussion with other people. I want to know where people see signs of the Spirit. I'll ask the various groups I work with this year. I need to see something real to sustain my hope — not something big, just something real.

There is a stirring within me — what, I am still not sure. The desire to move beyond the role of the critic to the task of creating something new? The desire to gather up my scattered energies and focus them in a deeper way?

*Holy Saturday, 1987*
Has it been spring or once again winter? Has it been only a month since Rachel's husband called me to say that she had only a few weeks to live? It had been a long time since we first met: he teaching the political philosophy classes which always adjourned to the Brunswick House tavern; she making her way as a gifted psychologist for women and children. I had started off admiring a gifted professor and had ended up friends with his earthy wife. Earthbound.

I went over to the hospital. At first she wouldn't see me — as she wouldn't see her husband or kids. None of us could understand it. She had always been so connected, so balanced. Within limits. And now the ultimate limit was there....

It was the shock of it all that made her freeze out those dearest to her. Thank God, I'm not so dear. Finally she agreed to see me. There was nothing that made sense to her. Although she knew the Jewish tradition, she hadn't believed in anything except those she loved. She was twitching with pain all the time. The only thing that calmed her was when I read the Psalms to her. From long ago, from far away, a voice echoed that stilled her spirit.

And then she died early in the morning of Good Friday. We put together a service at the gravesite because she wasn't really a synagogue type and her husband (a Christian) wasn't a church type. I read from Chapter 13 of Corinthians I: "Meanwhile, three things endure: faith, hope and love and the greatest of these is love."

But how she loved. Really. Today I was sitting in my room asking out loud, "Where has she gone?" And then I saw the yellow roses on my desk that someone had given me. And yes, I said, "There she is, in the yellow." I will never see yellow without thinking of Rachel.

...Her husband just called me. He said he had found her diaries and an entry from three months ago (when she didn't yet know she had cancer) said: "Psychology as a science is completely bankrupt. I must talk to Mary Jo about this." What did she know? What did her body know? Were the first signs of death entering into her subconscious or was this first admission of fallibility making itself felt in her body? Why didn't she call? What would we have talked about?

She is here now, in the yellow.

*May 3-5, 1987*
So here we are in Las Vegas — this greatest of gambling joints. What a paradox to be preparing for a civil disobedi-

ence action against nuclear testing in the shadow of Caesar's Palace! The great cosmic crap game! And we're gathering in this motel and preparing to go out to the test site—jukeboxes clanging and booze squirting. It's now clear that Bishop Tom Gumbleton has made a decision to cross the property line and be arrested. It's given profound hope to all those people who have been crossing the line for years. Strange how important it is for us that he has finally decided to do this. It's a line. Once you cross it you never come back. It's almost irrelevant that no other bishops have done this. Just one. Just one crossing of the line. That's enough to hope in.

...Out here in the desert I am almost numb with fear. They have told us of the hundreds of testings, of how the sand has turned to glass. Nothing ever, ever will grow here again. It's like a scene from the Apocalyptic writings: "the sea of glass". Here not even the stones cry out. And once again you feel yourself wavering.

RESISTING ILLUSIONS*
(CNT, May 31, 1987)

Four years ago, the American bishops issued a pastoral letter on peace which tested the moral metal of the church and the nation. In the furnace of these times, the people of God are purifying their position on peace.

Yet the government has continued to fuel the arms race. Its decision to prepare for war has been implemented many times over at the testing site in Nevada. The government has been tested beyond belief. And thus we are being tested—as human beings and as Christians.

---

* From the prayer reflections offered prior to civil disobedience action at the Nevada Test Site

Together we prepare to go into the desert—which has always been a place of testing. Like the people of Israel, like Jesus, we are being led into the desert—not to escape but rather to confront our illusions. The desert is a place where we are tempted by mirages, a place where truth is put to the test. We are being led into the wilderness like the early desert fathers who went there to test not only their personal illusions but also the social illusions of the declining empire that was Rome.

The empire that is America is now in a process of decline. America is in debt. It is no longer the economic centre of the world, and it is only a question of time before its loss of economic influence manifests itself as declining political power.

One of the clearest signs of the decline of this empire is the way in which America indulges itself in its illusions—illusions of apple-pie innocence and delusions of moral superiority. Another sign is the tendency to try to maintain its dominant position through the coercive use of power. It maintains the illusion of nobly building peace while it prepares for violent war.

The illusions of this declining empire are structured into this society in the form of elusive structures, as anyone who works for justice and peace issues knows. Once you feel the consequences of distant decisions on people's lives, then you begin to ask: "Who's responsible for this misery?" But this question only leads you into a world structured in circles—from door to door, desk to desk. As you move back and forth between the inner and outer circles of the structure, you keep circling around the question of responsibility. It is a dizzying round of denial. Nobody seems responsible.

We caught a brief glimpse of the elusive structures of a society formed by illusions at the Nuremberg trials after the Second World War. On the one hand, those who belonged to the Nazi inner circle claimed that they personally had never killed anyone; they had simply signed memos, filed away the lives of other human beings. On the other hand, those who worked in the concentration camps said that they were merely "following orders". Nobody seemed responsible.

The problem with a situation in which nobody seems responsible is that everyone feels guilty—but only vaguely so. Ironically, it is only those who are more morally innocent who try to struggle with the greyness of such guilt. We are all enveloped into the folds of the elusive structures of the empire. We are encircled by its fictions, as an elusive system maintains an appearance of solidity through propaganda, the device through which anything repeated often enough becomes true, regardless of the facts. A society conditioned to believe the illusion that "Coke is the real thing" will also believe that "the Bomb will set you free."

We are not up against a good old-fashioned hierarchical structure in which there are clear, albeit often unjust, lines of responsibility and accountability. We are encircled by structures which enshroud the manufacture of death.

It is difficult for us to adjust our minds and hearts to find the spirituality and strategies appropriate for shaping a Christian response within a shapeless and shifting structure. The left, for example, is often reduced to the old-fashioned game of searching out the villains responsible for evil in the world. This effort usually leaves them with the awkward task of explaining away the embarrassing fact that those they deem responsible are often rather nice people.

It is frightening to realize that most of the evil in the world today is being done by ordinary people who lose their sense of personal responsibility within the circular structures they work in. Ordinary people who simply do their jobs contribute cumulatively to the most extraordinary evils.

Let us see through the illusions of this empire without lapsing into our own delusions. Reagan is neither the saviour of the empire nor an evil man. Reagan is an illusion. But illusions are powerful. Illusions are dangerous.

In this desert time, we are called to resist the illusions of the empire. Yet a clear response to this call often eludes us. In the long struggle with the evasions of justice, we can become like what we are fighting against. We too are prone to self-delusion. What then? What now?

The road to resisting the illusions lies by way of the facts. Which facts? Not simply more facts about the horrors of global holocaust; it does seem that the more facts we know about nuclear weapons, the less we feel able to do. No, not this way.

We need to recover an even more basic fact—the fact of our life. Our resistance to the illusions of a dying empire begins with life. Our resistance to the elusive structures which enshroud the organization of death begins with a sense of awe about the fact of having been born. We tend to take the fact of our life for granted. We take the fact of our conception and birth for granted. Yet we "ain't necessarily so". There is all the difference in the world between being born and not being born. To dwell on this difference, to delight in it, is to open ourselves to the revelation that life is a gift. To contemplate this most obvious fact reveals the root of religious resistance.

Our Jewish ancestors collectively received such a revelation in the desert. When they left Egypt, they also left behind the illusion imposed on them by Pharaoh—the illusion that someone could make or break their lives. Yet in the desert they were tempted by another illusion—the self-delusion that they could manufacture their own lives.

When the effort to do so proved futile, they were more ready for the revelation that their lives were sustained by the One who created daily bread and caused water to flow from the rock. The facts of life in the desert were the grounds for their gratitude.

The desert was also a place of temptation for Jesus. There He confronted the illusion that, through things or others or self-possession, He could become a self-made man. In the end He resisted this illusion with the fact that His life was given by God. It was only a question of time before Jesus began to give His life away—as daily as manna in the desert.

We who live in a desert time must find the roots of our resistance in the revelation that begins with the fact of life. Those who know that life is a gift will resist the manufacture of death.

There is, of course, the kind of death which comes to us all as the natural end of our lives in this world. The religious person is called to meet this natural death with acceptance rather than resistance. Yet, in these times, it is all too tempting to accept humanly imposed death as almost natural. This is a dangerous illusion which must be resisted with solidity of spirit.

The desert is that space in our lives where we are called to resist the illusions that make life or death seem fictitious, or the mirages which blur the difference between life and death. The desert is that time in our lives when we act on the fact of our lives, when we become a factor in history.

The desert is not only a place of resistance. It is also the moment in which we discern what should not be resisted. It is the stretching space in which we encounter God as the irresistible One. Life and love and beauty and truth are the almost irresistible moments of manna in our desert times. Yet we are sometimes more tempted to resist love and life than violence and war. At those times, we reinforce our illusions and resist becoming who we really are — people for whom life is a blessing. Our resistance to illusions is only as tough as our willingness to tender ourselves over to the irresistible grace in our lives.

Jesus resisted neither God nor the lilies of the field nor the love of others. But He resisted the delusion of self-made salvation and the illusions of a declining empire. In the course of this resistance, He did not become elusive to Himself. His resistance to illusion was as clear as His transparent openness to God.

### THE APPEARANCE OF FORGIVENESS, THE REALITY OF JUSTICE*

Pope John Paul II's decision to grant an official audience to Austria's president, Kurt Waldheim, a man who lied about his Nazi past, has been interpreted by some as a papal gesture of forgiveness and reconciliation. This is a dangerous interpretation and reason enough to dispute this ill-advised visit. It compels us to comment further on the use and abuse of forgiveness in church and society.

Within the Jewish and Christian traditions, there is a deep sense that the motives within the human heart are known only by God. Thus, we withhold judgement about the motives of either the Pope or Waldheim in conducting this public meeting.

Yet, while it is difficult to judge why a person acts in a certain way, we can and must judge what a person does. Human beings, for better or worse, are responsible for the deeds they do. This responsibility for the consequences of

* Public statement issued by Mary Jo Leddy NDS, Carol Rittner RSM, and Professor Eva Fleischner, June 1987

our actions is grounded in the Jewish and Christian belief in the freedom and dignity of the human person. To deny this responsibility is to diminish the significance of all human actions. If we allow the passage of time to rescue a person (such as Waldheim) from the consequences of wrongdoing, then time will, in turn, rob human beings of the credit for the good they have done.

The evidence suggests that Waldheim's deeds during the Second World War must be brought to judgement. The Christian sacrament of reconciliation (which takes place only through the admission of guilt and repentance) was never meant to diminish the practice of human justice—which precisely in its moments of legal condemnation affirms the dignity of human beings in their freedom and responsibility.

In the confession of wrongdoing, the heart of the one who did wrong is healed. Yet wrongdoing wounds the entire human community, and it can be righted only by reinstating the dignity of persons and the community through just punishment. This is not vengeance. This is the vindication of human dignity.

Society must judge Waldheim's deeds. But who on earth can forgive him? Surely such an absolution ultimately lies in the hands of his victims, Jewish and non-Jewish. It would be presumptuous for us to forgive and forget in the name of Jews and non-Jews murdered by the Nazis.

Pope John Paul II gave the world a magnificent example of forgiveness when he visited Mahmet Ali Agca in prison. The Pope, who was the victim, forgave the one who had wounded him. The Pope, however, did not ask that Agca be released from prison, from the social consequences of his wrongdoing.

The Pope's meeting with Waldheim sets a very different and ambiguous example. Whatever the Pope's motives were in agreeing to such a meeting, a public appearance together at an official audience appears as absolving Waldheim from the consequences of his actions during the war and the Holocaust. It can easily and unfortunately be interpreted as part of the pattern of the church's denying the consequences that its own long history of anti-Semitism has had for the Jewish people.

*July 1987 (Our Lady of Peace Spiritual Life Center, Narragansett, Rhode Island)*
Came down to the ocean once again to do some writing, only to discover that this would be the last chapter in Kieran's life. She's in the hospital—on quadruple doses of morphine for the pain from the raging cancer. She is unconscious. But oh, how awesome she is. She is always praying from some point of herself that is most alive. Small prayers, short prayers—to God, with God. Now it's doubly clear—she wasn't just talking about God, she was with God, is with God.

It was as if she awoke (was it that the morphine had worn off just slightly or that there was one last message to send?) "I have a dream: I dreamt of all the men and women gathered around a table—all equal, all free. It will take a thousand years but it doesn't really matter. It will happen." And then the long silence.

And now I am left with a dream, a dream that I know is true. It's a dream about justice, equality, and peace. It's about the reign of God. And oh, it is true, it is true. It has come from the edge of night, spoken with words beyond words. It is true, it is true. And now I will say, day in and day out, somehow—the dream will come true.

She always said, "Trust your dreams." The wild Irish mystic—and I will, I will. And I will not be afraid.

*September 1987*
The Pope came back. He is fulfilling his promise to visit the native people of the north—since bad weather pre-

vented him from visiting them last time. So I am here on this little plane with the CBC-TV crew, flying on our way to hold a mirror up to this unusual event. What will there be to say except that he kept his promise, he did return to the people he'd promised to visit. Somehow promises seem so important to me now. There is so little that is promising—only the people who have promised themselves, risked themselves for the future. There is so little that is predictable. And how simple and sure such promises often are—like our promise to be together on New Year's.

*October 1987*
We are in the middle of nowhere in Appalachia—Odilie and I. A crazy pilgrimage that we decided to make after I had collected responses to my question "Where do you see signs of the Spirit?" After Rachel, after Kieran, after my awareness that we had been talking abstractly at *Catholic New Times* about a third option, I wanted to see for myself.

We could have gone anywhere but carved out a small section of country in the Midwest of the United States. My accumulated responses to the question had pinpointed about ten places on the map—except they weren't really on the map. As we travelled along on our three-week journey we discovered that most of them were on some out-of-the-way sideroad.

I realized how much of my life had been lived on the highway—where the signs are clear, the sustenance is sure, and you can go almost as fast as you want. You have to have good reason for getting off the highway. But here we are, and we both wanted it thus—she because she's from Central America and wants to believe there are "signs of the spirit" here, and I because it has now become a question I can't ignore if I'm to stay in North America....

The signs are small but they are sure. Little communities off the beaten track — up in the Smoky Mountains, down in the cornfields of the Midwest. Not many, but how it all adds up to the conviction that we (I?) must construct an alternative in the midst of this declining empire — some small but real dream in the midst of the nightmare that is named America.

A CHILD'S ADVENT IN SASKATOON
*(National Catholic Reporter* [U.S.A.], Dec. 1987)

The prairie sky coloured Advent pink throughout my childhood years. It is the colour that suffuses the sky in western Canada on the evening before a snowfall. We grew up out there seeing, above all, the sky — because there is so little else to get in its way.

As the land goes to sleep, the sky begins to awaken within us. Scrunching along in our snowboots on the way home from school, we were stopped in our tracks at the sight of the pink. The transformation of our cold and white world into a place of gentle light took our breath away.

Perhaps this helped us learn why to weather things, for Advent was when our snowtime life began in earnest. We took on the trappings of winter creatures and began to scurry along our beaten paths to school, to church, and to the homes of friends. We honed the skills that helped us survive the later wintry moments in our lives — how to see in the dark, how to keep our glasses from fogging over, how to keep one another warm.

We learned how to be at home in this winter world and, even more, how to play in it. Advent was the time we hauled out our skates, rubbed them with oil, and roared off to the neighbourhood rink. There, we would wobble and then wing on our way. The rink was a hard place of bumps and knocks and, sometimes, the clear ground of our most graceful moments.

We gathered pieces of cardboard from a local grocery store to build makeshift toboggans and trundled off to slide down the only real slope in the city — the bank of the Saskatchewan River. We knew this was a dangerous delight and all the adults had warned us about thin ice and the swirling currents underneath. The small river that snaked through Saskatoon was a symbol of some dark undercurrent in our lives. They told us many children had drowned in it. It was as if the only water they could trust was that which fell from the sky.

Advent seemed to coincide with the time the snow invited us to begin experimenting with shaping the world according to some image and likeness. We rolled out snowmen — not knowing then that there could be snow-women and snowpersons too! These figures were fat and friendly by nature. Lying down in the snow, we looked up at the sky and fanned out angels with our arms and legs. Growing up with a front yard full of friendly figures and angels traced all over the ground gives you a different perspective on life in the wider world. It makes it more difficult, for example, to imagine that other snowbound countries (such as Russia) are peopled only by men of ice and steel.

During this time of persistence and of playing, we prepared for the arrival of the Baby Jesus. Inspired by the ferverinos of our teachers, we made the daily sacrifices that became pieces of straw in the empty crib. Each morning, we puffed along our mile-long track to church, smoke steaming from our nostrils in the 40-below, to attend mass before classes began.

Years later, as I stood for days and nights in a long winter vigil outside a nuclear weapons plant in Toronto,

I thought of the persistent Advent piety I had grown into on the prairie. I realized that practice had stood me in good stead when the political chill of the 1980s made fidelity more important than success.

And there are moments when I search within myself for the warm heart of that child who would walk so far in such cold for the sake of another child.

Our parish always prepared for the annual Christmas pageant in a frenzy of excitement. Behind the curtains of the parish hall there were little squabbles, secret romances, and the usual tripping over the wires. But then the lights went on, our eyes all focused on the little Jesus, and we played out the story of love from long ago.

Our youth group always went carolling to various old folks' homes and hospitals in Saskatoon. It was the time of year I was forced to look into lonely eyes, into eyes seeing death rather than birth. As we walked from buiding to building, I felt as if the tears which had evaporated from someone in some silent other place were falling onto my cheeks as snowflakes.

This season was also the time my family was particularly aware of the fact that, in spite of the lights that bedecked our streets, life was not so bright everywhere else.

The phones began to ring at night with calls from a nearby Indian reservation—calls for my father, who was a surgeon. We kids would listen at the top of the stairs as he bundled up, warmed up the car, and drove off into the dark. Slowly I grew to understand how the onset of winter intensified the futility and boredom on the reserve to the point where many attempted suicide as a way of escape. For us, Advent was the sound of bells and of the phone ringing through the night.

One Christmas Eve (when I thought I had grown up), I felt the sights and sounds of all my childhood Advents give birth to a simple faith that remains as undeniable as the prairies within me.

That night, my novitiate companions and I were driving out to the small village near Saskatoon where we taught catechism on the weekends. The sky was pink and the snow was already starting to fall as we reached Colonsay. We opened up the little church and turned on the heat. That done, I settled back into the pew to wait. Then I heard the sound of small bells. Half wondering whether it was the angels, I walked to the door of the church and looked out over the fields. In the distance, I saw families in horse-drawn sleighs coming slowly through the prairie pink. It was as if the sky had sounded out the earth and found, once more, that it was very good.

*New Year's Day, 1988*
Death seems to have walked in and joined our party — an unseen and unwelcome guest. First there was the death of Christopher, then Rachel, then Kieran. And now Mark's mother and Isabel's father. We offered prayers for all of them.

Somehow, all of a sudden, we seem so fragile, so mortal. As I looked around at the group, I realized that we are, if not wiser, at least older. Mark's beard is beginning to turn grey, Ann has a middle-aged spread, Bill is just slower — can't manage the more intricate tunes on his guitar. I look in the mirror and see wrinkles. Margaret Brennan tells me she loves her wrinkles — each one has a name and a face. Maybe someday I'll love my wrinkles. Right now they're just wrinkles.

I brought along my copy of Etty Hillesum's diary (*An Interrupted Life*) to share some of the sections with the others. It seemed appropriate. There she was, a Jewish woman in the midst of the Nazi invasion of Holland, and she could still be amazed at the flower outside her window.

Have been struck by her insistence on the importance of building a "shelter" for our sorrow. This means: make room for it in your heart—don't deny it but don't absolutize it either. Sorrow must be given its due, its space and time.

I have some sense that my/our sorrow, the sorrow of the world, has a place of shelter in God's heart.

The people I have loved have each carved out a space in my heart—even when they die or go away the space remains, a space that no one else can fill. Someone new opens up a new space but never takes the place of those who are gone.

Eventually the mood of the evening changed. Bill had us all up clucking and flapping our wings as we danced "the chicken". Then I showed some of the slides of the places I had visited during my pilgrimage this fall. Lots of excitement. Lots of questions. I felt as if we were sharing "good news"—that there are people who are really living out an alternative to this culture. Jim was bothered by the fact that all the places I had visited seemed so far away from the mainstream. "We can't all just drop out and go back to the land. This ain't the sixties any more!" We don't need to be reminded of that.

The slides evoked some of the hope that can still be kindled at a moment's notice among us. Yet there was a certain wistfulness. For someone like Jim, there are realities that have redefined his hope—almost, but not quite. At one point in the evening, I thought the whole bunch of us were ready to go out and rent a van and take off for some unending sideroad in America.

A gift of the Christmas season: went to a performance of the Messiah at Massey Hall and found myself sitting next to Lois Wilson (former moderator of the United Church of Canada). It was awkward at first—we had had words at the time of the papal visit. We both became tribal — I was just a Catholic and she was just a Protestant.

Yet as we sat there the music seemed to draw us each into a gentler, more joyful part of ourselves. All the politics, all the issues, seemed to fade away and there we were — just two innocents listening to the story of the Prince of Peace as if for the first time. At the break we talked about our families, about what we were doing for Christmas.

### WHERE DEEP JOY MEETS THE
### DEEP HUNGER OF THE WORLD
### (CNT, Feb. 28, 1988)

Call it what you will — a nagging sense that one's life is not for nothing, a whisper that becomes the Word of one's life, a shot in the dark, a cry piercing through the chatter — a call.

Whatever shape it takes, there is a sounding out which takes place, at some moment, in the life of every Christian.

That moment may be fleeting and, perhaps, forgotten. However, it may also be the time when, like Jacob, we wrestle with our angel.

I have been with several people who have struggled, with simple grace or gutsy slugs, with the Messenger of their lives. At some point, they ask (in whatever words are theirs): "Is this an angel or a demon? Am I on the path of life or on the road to destruction?"

Call it what you will — the need for a divining rod, the fear of wasting what little there is, the sense of not knowing what is nonsense, the desire to discern God's will.

Face to face with those who want to keep an appointment with their call, I have often recalled the words of Monsignor Clem Kern, the man who was called "the saint of the slums" in Detroit: "The place where God calls you is the place where your deep joy meets the deep hunger of the world." The words of this holy man form a kind of crossroad of the ways which so often lead us in separate, and dead-end, directions.

He was a person with a profound sense that one could not find joy if there was a turning away from the hunger and suffering of the world. He understood that a response to the world's deep hunger must also be a deep joy, or nothing at all.

It is worth exploring each of these paths to see where they would end up if pursued in separation from each other.

There is so much in our culture which urges us to seek the way of personal joy by denying the deep hunger of the world. We live in a culture which preaches the creed of "me first" – the creed of consumerism, which militates against the gospel of Jesus. We all consume this creed daily, hourly, minute by minute, through the various forms of advertising. We are held captive by the illusion that what counts is me, here, now.

How easily such seductive illusions shape some of the popular spiritualities in the church: "First you have to find yourself before you can reach out to others." "We must know how much we are loved by God, by others, before we can love others."

There is, of course, a truth in the fact that we must be loved in order to love. But how easily in this culture that truth becomes false. We who accumulate many things, many experiences, many relationships, tend to think of love as something which must be accumulated before it can be invested or given away.

Strip away all the rhetoric from this kind of liberal spirituality and a view of the human person as a thing lies exposed.

From such a perspective, the person shrinks to the size and shape of something like a Coke bottle, which must be filled up before it can spill over its goods to others.

Is the mystery of life so easily measured out? Can the Coke-bottle person really say what it feels like to be half full or three-quarters full of love? Such a contained view of any person ignores the fact that the hunger to be loved (affirmed, cared for, appreciated) is an infinite and almost absolute hunger. Only the propaganda of a consumer culture preaches that such a hunger can, and should, be fulfilled. Here and now.

I cannot help but recall a luncheon I had with a young woman whom I knew quite well. She had everything the consumer culture counts as important: looks, talent, a well-paying career. She had everything that should add up on the liberal Christian ledger of personal fulfilment: many friends, a loving husband, and, at times, a profound sense that God loved her.

Yet she could sit across from me at the table and say that she still wasn't ready to have a child because she "wasn't sure enough of her own worth, so what could her child count on?" I was disturbed by her remark, not because she was neurotic but because she seemed so disturbingly normal.

Strangely enough, I became more aware of her dead-end route while I was reading the writings of John of the Cross, that sixteenth-century poetic mystic of Spain who chose not to avoid the political struggles of the church in his times. In the midst of darkness, within and without, he wrote: "Only the lover knows he is loved." It named something I already half knew.

Parents often have a privileged sense of what John of the Cross was talking about. They look on their small child and love him or her without reserve. This child is a joy — not because of the love it gives but because of the love it calls forth. This gurgling and helplessly messy bundle calls forth the love of those who gave it birth. Outreaching utterly, blind to themselves, parents can be freed by this love.

In this most simple and spontaneous experience of love, parents can understand from the inside what it is like for God to look on us small persons as little bundles of joy — loving us simply because we are. Parents can have a sense, as sure as smelly diapers, of how easy it is for God to love our unsanitized selves.

Not long ago, I watched an older sister watering plants by a window to the sun. For one brief moment, I saw her beauty illumined from within. It was impossible not to love her, freely and simply.

When we know how easily and freely we have loved another, we know enough to believe that we too are loved without reserve.

Only in loving do we know we are loved. We can do many things, give bits and pieces of ourselves, spend a lot of time and energy and money — and be without love. Only in loving is our deep hunger to be loved nourished. That is why the way of Jesus is one of boundless joy. That is why we eventually come to a dead end if we attempt to pursue our personal joy by leaving the hunger of the world behind.

Where are we led if we move to respond to the deep hunger of the world by turning our backs on our own desire for joy? The signs are written all over the faces of many of those who are involved in efforts of justice and peace — earnestness, grimness, sadness.

One can do all the politically correct and socially com- mitted things in the world and be without joy. Justice done without joy reduces itself to ashes instead of igniting the Spirit. Witness the number of good and generous people who have burned out in responding to the deep hungers of the world.

Why is this so? There are, perhaps, as many reasons as people, but some signal the dead-endedness of this way more than others.

It is an unfortunate fact that sometimes those who have become more conscious of the deep hungers of the world — for bread, for justice, for healing, for meaning, for love — remain less aware of their own deep hungers.

In responding to the various hungers in the world, one can also be feeding a deep personal hunger for affirmation, for significance, for the legitimation of anger. There is nothing inherently wrong about such mixed motives — motives are never pure this side of heaven. However, there is something dangerous in not being clear about where one's own hungers end and another's begin. Those who do become more conscious of their own hungers are sometimes able to place them in intentional solidarity with the hungering of the world.

It also seems that our response to the deeply hungry is often guided by guilt. Little wonder. It gets difficult to watch new footage from the Sudan and eat junk food. But while guilt may stop us from doing wrong, it does not start us doing good. Although guilt may result in a spasm of reaction, it eventually becomes an immobilizing cramp.

Paradoxically, the guilty awareness that one has too much is often accompanied by the deep fear that one is too little. The sense that others do not have enough often turns back on oneself as the sense that "I am not enough. We are not enough." And then we are stopped in our tracks.

Guilt does not nourish giving; it gnaws away at our souls, leaving us consumed.

My sense is that it is those who live out of a sense of gratitude, rather than guilt, who can respond to the world's deep hungers and not get eaten up in the process. Gratitude is the starting point for any life that is religious, yet it is the attitude we often seem to arrive at last. The basic religious attitude is not gratefulness for this or that thing, this person, that moment. It is the simple awareness that just being alive is an amazing grace.

The sense that one has been given the gift of life tends to turn one's life inside out — graciously, generously. While the guilty person measures life — who has more and who has less, who is better and who is worse — the grateful person does not count the cost because he or she dwells in a sense of the immeasurable.

The Jewish people have a wonderful prayer of gratitude which they recite during their Passover meal. In singing the story of their history with God, they remember each moment and say — if You had only done this for us, "it would have been enough." If You had only led us out of Egypt and not taken us through the Red Sea — "it would have been enough." They are grateful for reaching the Promised Land, but even if God had only taken them out of Egypt, "it would have been enough" to rejoice in for ever.

To speak the word "enough" in this culture is a radical act of political resistance. The creed of consumerism preaches that we have to have "more", "bigger" and "better". True believers of this creed can never have enough.

However, there are people such as Clem Kern in whom gratitude is so easily transformed into love for those who really do not have enough, who are too consumed by hunger to rejoice in the fact of being alive.

Because grateful people have a sense of having been given the one thing necessary, they are given over. They tend to give away what others see as essential and basic: things, money, prestige, job security, relationships, etc. It can seem as if they have nothing to lose. They care but they are carefree. They can't be manipulated by needs and wants. They choose to give of themselves and do not feel eaten up in the process. They know that, such as they are, they are enough. This simple belief starts them and sustains them in their response to life.

This is the way of Jesus, whose deep joy met the deep hunger of the world.


### THE OBEDIENCE OF THIS HOUR
### (CNT, May 1, 1988)

OTTAWA — April 14 has been a full day on Parliament Hill for the Japanese Canadians who have come to Ottawa. Joy Kogawa and I come in out of the rain and settle in over a warm cup of coffee at a small restaurant in the Sparks Street Mall.

We savour the moment. So many have come from all over the country to press their claim for redress with the government.

I remark at the dignity of the event that day. Joy explains that it is a big step for Japanese Canadians to march for their rights, that for every word spoken at the rally, there is much more left unsaid.

"In many ways we are a culture of silence. It was an honourable thing to suffer in silence."

I remember how it was through the words of Joy Kogawa that the silent sorrow of Japanese Canadians found eloquent voice. *Obasan*, her highly acclaimed novel, was the first many, like myself, had heard of the suffering of those who had been locked away in our nation's past.

Yet, staring at the glass of water on the table, she wonders if she has lost the gift of writing. The politics of organizing the Japanese Canadian community have so consumed her energies that there is little time left for poetry.

Joy reflects on how her life has unfolded over the past ten years. Like many who look back over their lives, she finds much she doesn't understand. Unlike most, she doesn't seem to need to understand at all.

Her life before the writing of *Obasan* was characterized by poetry — "which is a kind of discipline, a quest for interiority, the practice of sweeping the leaves along the avenue of the unconscious. It involves the practice of trust." The book marked the beginning of her shift away from poetry. "At some point I stopped writing poetry without even knowing it."

In 1978, she had a dream in which she was told she should go and work in the National Archives in Ottawa. She went.

Soon after she arrived, one of the librarians showed her a file of the correspondence of Muriel Kitagawa, a woman who had been interned during the war. "I knew I had to do something with this."

*Obasan* was written during 1978 and 1979. The first draft was written as poetry. "I trust in what is not yet conscious. This has sustained me through terrible doubts. At that time, I continued my obedience to the unconscious and to trust."

Her questions, in the course of writing a story located in the experience of internment, were not at all political or ethnic. "It was primarily a religious struggle having to do with good and evil, with the meaning of life."

The second draft of the book moved more towards prose. "That required a different kind of breathing. Poetry is like a gasp; prose demands a longer breath. It engages other aspects of one's being."

What finally emerged was a book in which the figure of the old woman Obasan was an internal voice "which is like mine, like my mother's, and the figure of Aunt Emily conveys a more conscious social voice of the type which was evident in the writings of Muriel Kitagawa. But I never had any feeling of political awakening as I was writing the book."

After the publication of *Obasan*, Joy became increasingly involved in promoting the cause of Japanese Canadians. "I have a sense of some of the blindnesses and pitfalls of politics and have experienced some of its passion. It's engulfed me. I am in danger of losing some of my poetry because of my political involvements."

Why doesn't she leave the political action to others?

"If there is a loss in my writing because of politics, I will continue to trust because there is nothing else I can do. This is the obedience called for this hour. What would my writing have gained, what would my poetry be worth, if I hadn't acted with those I love? My writing seems to be a calling but you never know. There are always other forms of obedience...."

Joy Kogawa begins to resemble the clear glass of water in the middle of our cluttered table.

I trace along the tablecloth with my spoon—feeling for some connection with the bumps in my own life. I wonder out loud about the serious concern some have that the church has lost its sense of mystery, its poetry, in engaging in its new-found political commitments.

What follows is not in the usual menu of answers: "One makes a decision. The only thing I can do is to do it with trust. If I make a mistake, I trust I will be pulled back. My soul is in safe-keeping."

Circling around with my spoon again, I share my conversation with one of the men at the rally, who says he tried to go to church during the war but was turned away from every church in town.

"There are many stories like that," says Joy. "Individual

people in the church did things to help us but as a bureau-cratic entity there was as much racism in the church as anywhere else."

Joy herself was held with members of her family at the internment camp of Slocan, British Columbia. That was when she was seven years old.

Her father, an Anglican priest, went to make an impassioned plea for support before the national synod of his church — but to no avail. These days Joy finds support in the people of Little Trinity Church in Toronto. "At the grassroots of the church there is a lot of hope." She is strengthened when others (in the church, in media, in public life) stand up and speak for Japanese Canadians.

"This enables the community to stand up. There is a crying in the community to know it is loved and valued. The amazing thing is that the community seems to have the capacity to receive the reality of love, of being loved, even after all that has happened. The love could be there and we could fail to see it. But the amazing thing is that we do see it."

The bill shows the price of coffee. The water is free.

*May 1988*
The issue of abortion keeps knocking at the door of my consciousness. And it plagues me through phone calls from the press. They want some token Catholic woman to say the hierarchy is wrong on this. They expect me to say the bishops are wrong. It's something I want to shut out. I tell myself again and again, "It's not my issue." Knock knock. Who's there?

Long talk with June Callwood — someone I could hardly admire more. We agree on every issue except this one. And in some ways I would rather march with her than with some of the crazies in the pro-life movement. I would rather march with her than with most of the bishops in this country. But there have always been crazies in the marches I've joined. The peace movement was always full of crazies I would never have wanted to be seen dead with.

June and I agreed on this: no matter who wins this awful battle over abortion, we are all going to lose the war — because of the violence that's been engendered on each side.

It's not my issue. And yet the phone calls from both sides increase every day. Are you for women? Are you for children? Knock knock.

...Once again the sense that I can't back off from this issue without backing off from myself — and so much more. Abortion has become the vortex that is drawing into itself many other issues.

I am haunted by the Holocaust, by the memories of a time when the powerful defined the weak out of existence. And I am grounded once again in the amazing grace of simply being alive. Christopher. If I choose to speak out of this I know I will be burning my bridges with the women I respect most. And I know I will be cast once again into the Catholic ghetto. And I know it will be for naught. I know that, in the end, we will probably have pro-choice legislation in this country.

Because...because...everything depends on our willingness and our ability to communicate this awesome sense of the grace of simply being alive. Somehow I think that someone who deeply senses this would never deprive any other person (woman or man) of this grace. But I hardly know how to speak (much less write) about this. It is a still, small grace.

And I know how often I have not lived out of this simple amazement. How can I condemn the women who are as much victims of this self-productive, often violent society as I am? How can I deny that the male-dominated church

I am part of seems more interested in producing kids than in loving one another? I want to write but can't find the metaphors for my simple sense: "Isn't it wonderful we are alive? Isn't it wonderful anyone is alive?" My words fail me as never before.

AN OPEN LETTER TO SOCIALLY CONCERNED
CATHOLICS: RESIST ABORTION NOW
(CNT, June 26, 1988)

As the House of Commons prepares to debate legislation on abortion, we appeal to all socially concerned Catholics to take up the profound moral challenge which confronts us at this time.

We are convinced that this is a decisive moment. How we respond to the call of this hour will significantly define the future of our society and of our church.

Our work at *Catholic New Times* has brought us into closer contact with socially concerned Catholics. Writing has been our way of serving various justice and peace efforts in the church. We have tried to communicate a scriptural vision of the social solidarity which promises justice for all — especially the most voiceless and power- less. Our commitment to solidarity is the political transla- tion of our faith in God, the Creator, who is Life that is shared by and for all.

As we have become increasingly critical of the values of liberal capitalism which have so shaped our culture, we have worked to strengthen a radical sense of church — one which is truly counter-cultural.

We are committed to resisting the world view of liberal capitalism and the parallel political perspective which sees society as a system of competing individual rights which must be legally bartered. This liberal world view is shared in varying degrees by all three political parties. It distorts a vision of social solidarity.

In our efforts to speak for a more radical church, we have been critical of some of the conservative tendencies in the church today. We have also tried to move beyond the merely liberal sense of church which seems preoccupied with spiritual self-development and personal prerogatives.

Thus, we are disturbed when we see Catholics, who advocate a more radical social solidarity on many issues, regressing to a popular liberal position on the question of abortion.

Some of this we understand but do not accept.

We understand those who have been put off by some in the pro-life movement who have reduced the concern for life to a simple anti-abortion focus. It is tragic to see how the finest efforts of many good people in the pro-life movement have been compromised by those in the movement who are also, for example, noisily in favour of capital punishment and nuclear arms. The disparaging attitude towards women, on the part of a few pro-life people, helps to discredit the movement even further.

Nevertheless, pro-life groups have borne the political heat of the day on the issue of abortion. And they have borne it with courage. In doing so, they have given to others the freedom to take on different, but related, searing social problems. In a time when moral considerations have grown all too cold and calculating, the passionate conviction of pro-life advocates is a welcome challenge.

Tolerant liberals, who find some pro-life tactics neither nice nor politically polite, would do well to examine whether there is any issue over which they would be willing to risk offending the current sense of what is socially appropriate. Appeals for tolerance become empty rhetoric when they attempt to talk away realities which are intolerable.

It would be disastrous, for our country and our church, if the social virtue of tolerance were invoked to legitimate the decertification of the unborn as human beings.

Our work for justice will be totally lacking in integrity if we, by omission or commission, participate in bartering away the rights of the smallest and weakest members of society.

We call on socially concerned Catholics to resist adapting to a social situation in which the rights of the weaker are defined by the stronger, in which the needs of the voiceless are determined by the articulations of the sophisticated, in which the social problems of the present overwhelm the possibility of future generations responding to them.

The increasing number of abortions is symptomatic of a culture characterized by diminishing expectations. We continue to hope in a more inclusive and interdependent society because, as Archbishop James M. Hayes has written, "for us to accept abortion would be to deny our hope in the future and to despair of our God-given capacity to transform those mentalities and social conditions which perpetuate injustice against women, against all persons." Abortion does not alleviate problems such as poverty and sexism but rather perpetuates them.

We agree with the archbishop's assessment that abortion is a dramatic example of a more general abdication of faith in the future. "The society which accepts abortion as a solution to present problems (whether personal or social) is also a society which abuses its children, lays waste the environment, risks nuclear war, and implements economic policies in which the immediate benefits to some will be dearly paid for by many in the future."

The pro-choice position undercuts the possibility of present and future social solidarity.

This is not to diminish the admirable social commitment of some who advocate a pro-choice position. This is not to deny the well-spring of mercy, within the Christian tradition, for those who have had an abortion. This is not to denigrate the concern of those struggling against the socio-economic conditions which have so limited the range of options open to women. Yet we do not believe that the rights of women, of any group, will be secure as long as the rights of one group can be negotiated out of existence. A society which assumes the divine right of deciding when life begins will all too easily move to deciding when life should end and for whom.

There are those who will say that church officials cannot speak effectively about abortion because of the patriarchal bias in the history of the church. And it is true that the church has a long way to go before becoming a credible advocate for women. It is also true that the church has much to learn from what is best in the liberal tradition.

Yet we are convinced that the church's stand on abortion is simply true. It speaks with prophetic clarity in the midst of the murky morality of liberal capitalism.

There are many important pieces of legislation which the government will be tabling during this long, hot summer. The debates over free trade, refugees, and the Meech Lake Accord will, for example, dramatically alter the future shape of our country. We must enter these debates with competence and care. Yet we must not allow the urgency of these debates to deflect us from realizing that the fundamental basis of social solidarity will be determined by the decision on abortion.

If we do not take a clear and determined stand on abortion now, we will soon find that the ground for all our efforts at social justice has disappeared from under our feet.

In the long run, our commitment to life demands our involvement in the process of transforming those economic conditions and social attitudes which have made abortion seem necessary.

However, this broader and longer commitment does not excuse us from facing the fact that our politicians are now discussing legislation which would make abortion not less necessary but more possible.

We are faced with a question of life and death. This question is here. It is now.

Let us not be naive. Pro-choice groups are organized and effective. They have enormous political access and influence, far exceeding their numbers, with members of Parliament and the Senate.

Over the years, the position of *Catholic New Times* has been clearly pro-life. However, we have not spoken strongly enough or often enough. We underestimated the political influence of the pro-choice lobby and overestimated the resources of the pro-life movement to carry the burden of this struggle. We also underestimated the moral plasticity of the consumer culture which was so easily reshaped after the decision to partially legalize abortion twenty years ago. We were mistaken in our judgement. We suspect we are not alone in having been so. Now is the time to speak and to act. To wait is to risk joining the cultural silence and numbness which threatens to engulf us all.

In the name of God, do something: go to the phone and call your member of Parliament. Walk a picket line. Commit civil disobedience. Wear a button. Start or join an action group. This is politics, and pressure is now what counts. Pressure the members of Parliament. May they not rest in peace.

*Signed:* The editorial committee of *Catholic New Times.*
Larry Colle, Mary Jo Leddy NDS, Frances Ryan OSU, and
Janet Somerville.

## July 1988

A marvellous and unexpected opportunity to sit in on
some classes given by liberation theologian Gustavo
Gutiérrez at Boston College. He's a tiny person with a
slight limp. I have been overwhelmed by the obvious holiness of the man. He is a grateful person — amazed, even
in the midst of the struggle of the poor, at the gratuity of
God's love. The reality of the man is so much more than
the caricatures of the "Communist theologian" painted
by the right wing.

A striking statement: "If you are seriously working for
justice and truth you will have many enemies. Expect
that and don't be surprised. But you will also have many
friends." And it's true. I have good friends.

### BEYOND NAGGING: THE PROPHETIC ROLE
### OF WOMEN IN THE CHURCH
### (CNT, Nov. 6, 1988)

Smack in the middle of the gospel of Matthew we find the
story of Jesus and a nagging woman. This story, so the
biblical commentators tell us, is of central importance in
the narrative of Matthew. It is the story of an encounter
in which there is a change of consciousness in the partici-
pants — not only in the woman but also in Jesus himself.
Through the nagging woman Jesus comes to a fuller sense
of His vocation, and through Jesus the Canaanite woman
is drawn to a deeper sense of her own call.

Let us imagine what Jesus might have said to himself when confronted by this nagging woman.

– This old Canaanite woman is a real pest.

– She is not one of the chosen yet she is choosing to come to me, she is looking for life, for her daughter but also for herself. If she is choosing life, how can she not be chosen?

– This woman says her daughter is possessed but she too is possessed by her daughter. She wants to possess her daughter and she wants to possess me.

– She wants to use me, just as she has learned how to use many men. She has learned how to survive in a world of men, how to nag, how to whimper and whine and beg. She has learned how to manipulate so that she herself will not be used. They say that is what women have to do to get what they want in a world of men. She wants to use our God, just as she has used idols – and been used by them.

– Yet she is nagging because she loves her daughter, wants her to live more than she wants to possess her. She is willing to seek beyond the idols of her tribe for the sake of her daughter.

– She wants her daughter to be more than her daughter just as my mother was willing to let me be more than her son.

– How would my mother have responded to this woman? I don't know, she never told me what to do....

– But I don't know what to do because I don't know who I am called to be.... Who do people say I am? Some say I am sent to the house of Israel...but this woman is a Canaanite.

– Yet...she wants her daughter to be more than her daughter just as my mother was willing to let me be more than her son. Can I see my God, our God, as more than our God? I would have to let myself be more than a prophet of my people. I would have to let myself be more than myself.

– No wonder this woman is so irritating, so disturbing, so challenging, so prophetic.

The Canaanite woman was prophetic in calling Jesus to a transformation of consciousness about his own vocation. If that is impressive, it is equally impressive that Jesus was able to hear a prophetic message in the persistent nagging of this woman.

The contemporary parallels to the story of this encounter are not too difficult to draw. We are hearing more and more about women pestering the church to move beyond its limited sense of itself—pestering for the sake of their daughters and themselves. Women are saying, "We want our daughters to live, to live fully in the church, and we want to bring our lives fully into the church."

The church has a choice now, as Jesus did then— between dismissing such woman as pests, or listening to the nagging questions raised by women and hearing in them an invitation to respond to its own vocation more fully.

How often the "official church" sees women as pests rather than prophets. There are many reasons for this dismissal of women as irritants, but one reason is the inability of many of us to recognize the prophetic voices in our midst.

Most of us share a rather stereotypical view of the prophet: the beardy-weirdy with eyes blazing and voice booming, "Thus saith the Lord." Yet this caricature hardly fits the descriptions of the prophets which we find in the sacred scriptures. They came in every shade and stripe: rich and poor, young and old, poetic and pragmatic. All of these were quite different, but alike in that they were chosen from among the people, for the people, with a certain message for a specific situation.

The fact that prophets are defined as such by the call to address a certain situation could lead us to a rather shocking realization—that prophets are not born but become prophets when called. Being prophetic is not a personality trait that some are born with and others are not. Being a prophet is a temporary assignment.

This should help all of us in the difficult and ongoing task of discerning between true and false prophets.

We can begin to sense the falseness of so-called prophets when they act as if they have something to say about every situation or issue.

We must question our own sense if we deny the prophetic truth a person has spoken in one situation because we know that what he or she says about another situation rings false.

If we read the reports of prophets in the scriptures, we see that they appear for only as long as their message is significant for the community. We do not read about them before or after the situation that called them forth and defined them. No one possesses the gift of prophecy for ever. It possesses us—sometime, somewhere.

The story of the Canaanite woman has become part of our Christian tradition because of the prophetic message she spoke in a certain situation, for a moment. Who she was and what she did before her encounter with Jesus was surely important to others and to God, but it is this moment that we remember and recall. Her encounter with Jesus was her prophetic moment.

I believe each of us has a prophetic moment...sometime, somewhere.

If the realities conveyed by the scriptures refuse to support our illusions about the prophets as some special race of people, why do we cling to such illusions?

Perhaps it is a way of protecting ourselves, a way of denying the possibility that we too may have one or two or three prophetic moments in our lives.

As long as we can believe in the illusion that prophets are few and far between, we can relax for the rest of the time – which is most of the time. As long as we continue to imagine today's prophets as beardy-weirdies or old hippies, we don't need to face ourselves or the situations in which we find ourselves.

Perhaps we continue to deny the possibility of prophetic moments in our lives because we know, on whatever level of consciousness, how prophets are dealt with in the church.

The "conservatives", who attempt to manage what they see as disorderly, tend to marginalize and denigrate the prophetic element in the church. The persecution of prophets may be quite subtle – sometimes they are simply stoned to death with popcorn.

The "liberals", who want to protect not so much the church as themselves, are far more subtle in their dealings with prophets. They say, "I respect your feelings and ideas and I expect you to respect mine." It's a sort of terminal tolerance.

Yet I know that some people, sometimes, somewhere, recognize a prophetic moment in their lives. I am still pondering why this is so but I do know that it is.

Most of my energies with *Catholic New Times* have been strengthened by the witness of those who heard a call to become prophetic at some moment in their lives. I recall the story we did about a grandmother pursuing a case to the Supreme Court that would allow taxpayers to sign over that portion of their tax money going to the military to a peace education fund; the story of Joy Kogawa, who followed a dream to the archives and so came to write about the sufferings of Japanese Canadians; the story of the Irish moss harvesters of Miminegash, P.E.I., who fought not only for their own economic rights but also for the people of the Philippines who shared in the same type of labour.

My own experience is a small "ditto" to the collective experience of our ancestors in the faith and of brothers and sisters today. On the basis of my limited experience, I would say that prophetic moments arise rather quickly and then pass us by if they go unrecognized. How often I have said: I should write something about this; I should do something about this. But then the moment passes and it doesn't seem to matter anyway.

Once or twice I think I have recognized such a moment and known I *had* to do something, to say something. Why? I don't know, really. A visceral grace. I do know that the one or two prophetic moments that addressed me were the ones I felt least prepared to deal with. As I recall, one of the most critical decisions we had to make at *Catholic New Times* had nothing to do with any issue within my range of competence and passion. It had to do with apartheid in South Africa. This was many years ago, long before *Cry Freedom* and the like. Why did we take on a very risky series of articles? I don't really know. It just seemed that we could no more not do this than not be ourselves.

A visceral grace. Perhaps that's why I feel drawn, again and again, to the story of the Canaanite woman and her prophetic moment.

The story in the gospel of Matthew is that of a woman who responds prophetically in the course of her encounter with Jesus. She becomes a liberating person because she is liberated in her deepest self — in that space where she has internalized the patterns of oppression in her culture. Let us imagine what this woman might have said to herself as she faced Jesus:

– My daughter is possessed. She doesn't know it but she is possessed: by things, and she is treated like a thing; by persons, and she becomes less of a person; by idols, and she becomes more servile.

– She is possessed by all the things and all the persons and all the idols that have possessed me. I have been the much-loved possession of my husband and family. I have been wrapped up in the package of patterns in my culture.

– How can I help my daughter when I have been so possessed...and my mother before me? Being possessed is a way of being that we have passed from generation to generation. It has become a habit of being, so familiar that I now cling to my daughter as my personal possession.

– Am I the demon that is possessing my daughter? Can I help her? Do I want to? Who would I be if I didn't possess her? Who would look after me in my old age? Who would mother me then?

– Yet I want her to be more than my daughter and I want to be more than her mother. We are both possessed by a familiar demon and long to be set free.

– I cannot be set free in Canaan, where I have become habituated to the pattern of possessiveness. But I have heard of a Jewish man who casts out demons. They say he is not possessed by anyone or anything.

– I call out to him: "My daughter is severely possessed by a demon." He doesn't answer. Maybe he would answer if he heard the depths of my cry: I am the possessed one who has possessed her. I must be set free in order for her to be set free. I want her to be different from me. I don't want her to have to nag her way through life.

– I look into his eyes and I see that this man too is possessed and needs to be free in one last way. He needs to be freed from the limits of his own idea of God...whom he calls "Father".

– I say to him: your father is more than you think, just

as I am more than my daughter thinks. You must let go of your self-possession.

– He calls me "woman": not mother of my daughter; not daughter of my parents or of my people; not wife of my husband, not old woman, not nagging woman, but— woman. With this person I know that I am a woman, and even more than a woman.

This is the story of a woman who became prophetic because her spirit was liberated. She was a woman whose creative power was set free as she discovered her deepest identity through this encounter with Jesus. She discovered that she was of God, with God, for God.

We can imagine that, after this encounter, nagging ceased to be her only way of life. She would speak with a clear voice, with her own voice. Her voice would no longer be that of a victim but that of a liberator.

There are many levels on which the liberation of women can and should take place. It is important for us to understand how spiritual freedom is ultimately related to the important work of socio-economic liberation and psychological liberation.

The struggle for equality in terms of jobs, wages, and opportunities is the beginning of the possibility of women finding their own voice. Without such liberation, women will continue to be economically de-energized, socially servile, and politically disempowered.

Without such liberation, women will continue to be passive and silent or will take out their aggression on those who inhabit the constricted world they have been consigned to. They will continue to nag. They will pick away at their small world.

As long as women are denied real political equality, they will find the range of their political power reduced to the conduct of wars and truces in personal relationships.

Their form of political discourse will remain at the level of gossip.

We are beginning to see real change in the socio-economic and political oppression of women. It is slow but it is getting surer. Much of this change has come about through the efforts of women who have chosen not to remain silent. Some nag, others speak more clearly...but they are not silent.

The sad truth, however, is that many women still remain silent and passive even when the possibility of social equality begins to open up before them. On a psychological level, they prefer the painful patterns of victimhood that they know to the responsibilities of equality which they do not know. They continue to set up oppressors over themselves even when there are no real ones in sight.

When we acknowledge this dynamic, we become more aware of the depth of liberation called for if women are to be truly free. Ultimately, the desire to choose life and the decision to act on that desire is a grace.

Jesus Christ is the liberating grace of our belief that life is stronger than death. He is the promise that we can be free from the deadly patterns within ourselves, within our society, and within our church. This was his prophetic message. His life, death, and resurrection give weight to his words.

We hear about the good news of the liberating grace of Jesus through our church community. The story of the Canaanite woman lies within the Word of God which is read and commented upon within our church community.

Unfortunately, some within the church do not seem to have taken the story of the Canaanite woman to heart. They do not seem to hear the nagging questions of women in the church today. They seem to prefer the silent women to the women who come to speak about the spiritual distress of their daughters, who are beginning to find equality everywhere but in the church.

Let us be clear about the reason for this distress: all the beautiful statements about the dignity and equality of women will ring hollow as long as ordination is the prerequisite for having a voice in the church. Even if very few women want to be ordained at the moment (especially when they see how priests themselves are so easily silenced), many more women are asking to be heard.

This is a prophetic moment for us as women in the church. Those of us who hesitate to speak for ourselves should think about our daughters. Let us not grumble among ourselves. Let us go and pester those who would keep us silent and say: we are trying to speak about life, we are beginning to sing a new song to the Lord.

Let us not go to ask permission to speak with our own voice. Let us go to offer the church the possibility of speaking the Word of God more authentically.

We can take courage from the story of the Canaanite woman. In it we find the reason for our hope that church officials will hear the nagging reality of women and will recognize their call to become more truly servants of the gospel of Jesus Christ.

This is a prophetic moment for the church.

*New Year's Day, 1989*
Luigi rolled into the party — and I mean rolled! Is he fat, or what! He says it's all part of his disguise — his bishop was suspicious of priests with a lean and hungry look. It seems the disguise didn't work — Luigi was booted out of his parish but he has landed on his feet working with one of the refugee agencies in Central America. He spent some time in Guatemala on his way back to Canada. It's hard to imagine the unrelenting terror he describes. "You just have to stop worrying about staying alive," he said.

It made me realize how much of what passes for life here is really just survival. I was surprised at the change in my attitude towards the struggle to survive. A few years ago, survival seemed like a moral imperative as we seemed on the brink of nuclear war. And I sensed that survival had been an ultimate act of faith during the Holocaust. But now things are less extreme — especially after Gorbachev's breathtaking moves. Now survival seems just "mere" survival — keeping on keeping on.

Mark and Ann both said they felt their communities had opted for survival, security. I tend to agree. Something about this kind of option is so morally debilitating. Choosing not to die is not the same as choosing to live.

Isabel has lost her job at the college because she questioned the judgement of the dean — again. How strange that she, the least contentious of all of us, would get fired. She's looking unemployment in the eye and hasn't blinked. Luigi says she should go to Latin America: "No unemployed theologians down there — dead, maybe, but not unemployed."

Isabel just smiled. She's not afraid. She's faced her own personal demons more honestly than most of us during the years she spent in therapy — faced her demons and made friends with them. She's not afraid.

And I am afraid. Of what? Of whom? The truth is, I'm afraid of dying — in any number of ways. Kieran is right. Luigi is right. I will not be free until this fear loses its power.

And I hear a voice from last night's supper, from the last supper, saying: "Do not be afraid. Do not be afraid."

*January 1989 (El Salvador)*
I was profoundly moved at the sight of the tombs of the two Maryknoll sisters who are buried with their people in the cemetery of Chalatenango. Just two simple graves,

resting here in El Salvador instead of back home in the States. Someone had left plastic flowers in a Campbell's soup can on the graves.

The women seemed so close as we were driving in to the capital from the airport along the dark road where they had been raped and murdered. I was terrified. An army truck followed us along the road from the airport — rifles trained on our car windows. The first terrified impression has continued. Kids with guns everywhere. You could die here for no reason — just some kid's whim. And there are lots who are killed for a reason.

AND DEATH SHALL HAVE NO DOMINION
(CNT, Feb. 5, 1989)

SAN SALVADOR, EL SALVADOR — There are children in El Salvador who grow up learning the facts of death before they learn the "facts of life".

One such child is the son of Miguel Angela Montenegro, a leader in the Human Rights Commission of El Salvador (CDHES).

The son wandered into the documentation room as Miguel was showing a group of us the "evidence" of human rights abuse in that country. The commission's work of the previous day had already been developed into photographs and recorded on videotape. There, in black and white and colour, were the bodies of two young men: one had been decapitated, his testicles mutilated. The other showed different signs of torture; the fingers of his right hand had been cut off.

As I gasped for air, Miguel's young son began to look at the photos on the table. The father made no attempt to hide this brutal reality from him.

Early childhood educators elsewhere may shudder at

all of this. Neuroses. Psychoses. Not healthy. Not happy. What will this child grow up to be?

If he becomes the man his father is, he will be a Christian.

Miguel, compact and clear, was a revelation to me of the depths of the Christian mystery which is being lived out in El Salvador. Somehow, he has gone beyond his fear of death. Because he has died before he dies, he has become one of the liberators in this land dominated by the terror of death.

On the walls of CDHES, in the modest two-storey house which is both home and office to members of the commission, are the photos of seven members of the organization who have been assassinated since its founding in 1978. One of the photos is of Dr. Marianella García Villas, president of the commission until her assassination in March 1983. Her tortured body was found dismembered.

"It was Marianella who got me involved in the commission," says Miguel.

The most recent photo is of Herbert Anaya, murdered in October 1987 while taking his children to school. The words below the photo develop a picture of Anaya's soul: "The agony of not working for justice is stronger than the certain possibility of my death; this latter is but one instant, the other is one's whole life."

Miguel carries on, taking up the refrain of those now silenced. For him, as for others, death is a certain possibility. Not death from natural causes but death which is humanly organized and executed.

Most of Miguel's relatives have been murdered. He has already been arrested and tortured. He has been the recipient of numerous death threats. Friends and supporters have offered him airfare out of the country and a safe place for his family, his wife and four young children.

"I am sick and tired of threats against my life. We will continue our work."

Why? How?

"People come to us and ask us not to abandon them. We won't abandon them. Those who suffer fill us with strength and hope. We know we are not alone. We are confident you will not leave us alone.

"Are we afraid? Of course we are afraid. Every human being is afraid of dying. But if we are ruled by fear we will do nothing."

The whole military and political apparatus in El Salvador rules by fear. Terror as a tactic takes many forms — harassment of civilians, the military "operations", the destruction of property, the destruction of body and soul.

It works — but not always.

Sometimes, in some places, in some people, death no longer has dominion.

There are others who, like Miguel, have lived their fear until the fear blinks at life.

There are the refugees who decided to leave the camps in Honduras and to return and rebuild their villages in El Salvador. Their story is a concrete, contemporary parallel to the Exodus story. These people left their place of captivity and returned to their land in spite of threats from the military and the seductions of the government to settle elsewhere. They knew it would not be easy back home in El Salvador but, as one woman explained to me, "We were suffering anyway in Honduras so we decided we might as well suffer for something meaningful."

Old Gregorio, who was part of the first group to leave the Mesa Grande camp in Honduras, has a story to illustrate the perils of timidity.

"There was a woman who had a bowl of food in front of her but she was afraid to eat because she didn't have a spoon. She waited until someone gave her a plastic spoon. But it broke and she choked on it."

Then there is the story of the people in Chalatenango who pelted soldiers with tomatoes and eggs as they chased a man through the marketplace.

Stories such as this lead a priest working with small Christian communities to explain why fear loses its hold at times. "Anybody can die just walking around in El Salvador. The poor know they are going to die anyway so it might as well be for a good reason."

The desire to live freely, to live meaningfully, robs death of its power. For some in El Salvador, a chosen death is preferable to mute submission to the murderous machinery of terror. It is a choice that promises liberation not only for oneself but also for others.

It is a resurrecting choice, one which was made by Archbishop Oscar Romero, whose spirit still hovers over this land. Speaking two weeks before his murder, he said, "I have often been threatened with death, but as a Christian I do not believe in death without resurrection. If they kill me I will rise in the Salvadoran people."

The words of Miguel, Herbert Anaya, and Oscar Romero speak of deep freedom. They are the words of those who are free to live and free to die.

There is a great deal of propaganda about "freedom" in El Salvador these days, especially as the election draws near. In the name of democratic freedoms, the United States is pouring two million dollars a day into this country to prop up the façade of freedom. In reality, this "freedom" is merely licence for the few. Sometimes it becomes a licence to kill.

Nevertheless the cycle of fear, of destruction and degradation, is broken by those liberators who have died before they die. Their resurrection and that of their people begins even now.

Marx was only partly right when he criticized the religious belief in life after life as being "the opium of the people". There are times and places, extreme situations, when only a life directed by faith in some kind of resurrection can liberate people from the domination of death.

Such extreme situations should never be accepted as normal—for oneself or for anyone else. Yet these situations cannot be rejected as being outside our human or Christian experience.

What does this mean for those of us who live in El Norte?

Here death comes more naturally and life becomes more artificial. Mostly, we just survive—choosing not to die but not choosing to live. We keep on keeping on. We prop up our façades of freedom and erect defences against death. Some of us are too busy to die and too busy to live.

If I have learned one thing from people like Miguel, it is that we have a choice between squandering our lives or sacrificing our lives.

That choice makes a difference in this world.

### "WHEN WE CAME HOME, EVEN THE CHICKENS WERE HAPPY"
### (CNT, Feb. 19, 1989)

There is a story told in El Salvador these days which echoes a story from another time and another place. It is a story written in people's hearts and handed on by word of mouth.

It is the remarkable story of the return of thousands of refugees from the camps in Honduras to their villages in El Salvador. Those who tell this tale use biblical words to relate the deep meaning of this experience—words like "exodus" and "return from captivity".

There is as yet no authorized version of the return which began in October 1987. There are facts and feelings and fillings-in. And there is faith — strong enough to move the mountains in this volcanic country.

One must listen long and low in the soul.

In many ways this remains an unfinished story. It is about beginnings, small but sturdy beginnings.

It is difficult to locate the first chapter of this story. Some would say it begins with the massive repression in the late seventies during which thousands of Salvadorans were slaughtered and countless people were driven from their homes and land. Many crossed the border into Honduras, where they were contained in three refugee camps: Mesa Grande, San Antonio, and Colomoncagua.

Others would say the story really begins in these places of captivity — for the refugees quickly learned that the soldiers of the Honduran military were their captors rather than their protectors.

Then came the cry of the people that was to last for eight years. The cry came from Egypt, from Babylon, from Honduras.

These people had already borne a great deal of suffering, but there was a new dimension to this suffering in the camps on the border. One young man explained it this way: "We suffered in El Salvador when we were trying to build a better life. Now, in the camps, we realize we still suffer but in a more painful way. We suffer for nothing. We suffer without hope."

Parents began to worry that their children would never see the rivers of El Salvador. The old people did not want to die in a strange land. Younger people felt diminished by the lack of work.

Nevertheless, they found the time and space in these crowded camps to reflect on the stories in the scriptures.

Many of the refugees had been active in small Christian communities in El Salvador and that involvement had been the cause of their persecution.

Arturo is clear about the threat a Christian consciousness posed to the status quo in El Salvador. "They didn't kill us just because we were in the way. They killed us to kill our belief that we are created by God and therefore we deserve a better way of life."

As the refugees listened to the stories of the scriptures, they also began to hear the news that some of the "internal refugees" (those who were in camps inside El Salvador) were trying to go back to their villages. Some of the refugees in Mesa Grande took heart at this news. "If our brothers and sisters inside El Salvador are going home, why can't we?"

At the same time an international commission, formed to deal with the refugees on the border, offered them three alternatives: 1) to become citizens of Honduras; 2) to go to a third country; 3) to return to El Salvador—but not to their villages.

This good news and bad news galvanized the people in the camps. People who had come from the same villages began to meet over a period of several months. Quite simply, they decided their own alternative. They wanted to go home. "We wanted a future," says Ernesto, "if not for ourselves, then for our children."

It wasn't that Pharaoh let them go—they let Pharaoh, the Pharaoh of fear, go.

"The Exodus was a story we had read but hadn't had a chance to finish," recalls Rosita.

The decision was grounded in a sense of the harsh realities they would be returning to. For Rosita it was "a necessary night to arrive at a new day; a necessary and difficult path to arrive at our promised land; a necessary hassle."

In January 1987, the refugees wrote President Duarte of El Salvador informing him of their intention to go home. They also announced their intention to the country through an advertisement in a national newspaper.

Then came the time of temptations. The military commander of El Salvador said the refugees would be in danger if they returned. They said they were going home.

President Duarte wanted them to wait six months. They said, "We are coming now."

The president said they could come back, but to places chosen by the government. They said, "We are going home."

The president said they could come back one by one. They said, "Alone we are too vulnerable but together we can make it."

Rumours began to circulate that the government would not allow food supplies into the villages. Old Gregorio shrugged off the threat: "Well, if we starve to death, at least we'll die quietly!"

Finally, faced with the determination of the refugees, President Duarte decided that it had been his idea all along and that it was a good example of how El Salvador was co-operating with the Arias Peace Plan for Central America.

At the last minute, the United Nations representatives said they could not provide transportation for the journey. The people said they would go on foot. The trucks did arrive, and on the tenth of October 4,313 people left the Mesa Grande camp. In three days they were home.

The statement of one older woman captures the joy of that moment. "When we came home even the chickens were happy!"

In villages like Santa Marta, Copapayo, Las Vueltas,

and Guarjila, the people began to uncover old wells and clear away the wreckage of war. It was hard work as they were mostly women and children and old people. But after many years of neither sowing nor reaping, these people again held the land in their hands.

They decided to work their land together. "It's stupid to look after your own land alone," explains Maria Luisa. "If you get sick it doesn't get harvested. When we work together, if one person gets sick the land is still looked after."

They are planting seeds of promise. However, these people know that this is not yet the Promised Land.

The military treats the villages as nothing more than potential food depots for the leftist guerrillas. Helicopters bomb the fields and military blockades are set up to prevent food and medical supplies from reaching the villages. Land mines in the countryside have made the sight of young children on crutches a familiar one. There are a thousand forms of harassment. One example: soldiers forced three men to eat grass and to sit on an ants' nest for hours.

The villagers must also cope with the seeds of suspicion sown by the military through their practice of paying people to inform on each other. A health worker in one village said that one of his tasks was to help those with psychological problems associated with the war. "Some people are very depressed. They have trouble with eating. One woman had a headache for eight years."

In spite of all of this, more people are returning home. In August 1988, another 1,200 people left Mesa Grande. A further group of 837 made their journey in November 1988. These groups, like the first group, were accompanied by "internationals" — people from other countries who acted as a kind of human buffer to protect the refugees on their way home. Together they parted the waters.

International solidarity is a crucial dimension of the hope of the repopulated villages. One priest who works in the villages described the internationals as "the umbrella which keeps away the rain".

This is an unfinished story. It is a story about beginnings, about small beginnings as stubborn as the Salvadoran people.

## Ephemeral Material*

He was a messenger of sorts, unannounced, unwelcome, ever-present.

I had seen him often — at almost every public address I had given, at every peace rally, at many a meeting on justice and human rights. He was always there — in his nondescript tweeds, beige hair, and beige trenchcoat. He had blended into the background of my public involvements over the last fifteen years.

He took it all in with the tape recorder in his half-open briefcase. We began to refer to him as "our friendly local spy". We were too busy planning and protesting to object to his presence among us.

If it hadn't been for the numbing boredom of a certain peace meeting last week, I might never have given him another thought.

I was perusing the walls, the floor, and the faces of those at the meeting when I noticed the friendly local fixture once again. His hand had just reached furtively into his briefcase. Then and there I resolved to find out the true colours of this little beige man.

At the break I went over to him and introduced myself. "I've seen you at these meetings for years," I said

* Draft for an unpublished article

pointedly. "I want to know who you are and what you're doing with that tape recorder in your briefcase. There's nothing secret or seditious in what we are doing."

He blushed. The first sign of colour. "Oh," he stammered, "my name is Arthur Brown and I work for the Metro Toronto Library. My job is to collect ephemeral material."

When I asked him what he meant by "ephemeral material" he said it was "talks, flyers, small newspapers, and things like that."

I returned to my seat somewhat shaken. Ephemeral material! What would be worse, I wondered — to discover that he was for real and that most of what I had been doing could be classified as "ephemeral material", or to find out that he belonged to the shadowy world of spies?

The next morning I called the library and they told me that there was indeed a section for "ephemera" but that no such person worked for them. I haven't seen the messenger since then.

*September 1989 (Wurtsmith Strategic Air Command Base, Michigan)*
It has been a privilege to be here this weekend. (Was invited to give the retreat reflections.) The people from Michigan who are preparing for the civil disobedience at the SAC base are a tried and true lot. Mostly just ordinary middle-class folk. Unlike some in the peace movement, they're not acting out unresolved childhood stuff with the law and authority. And they really know how to have fun.

Somehow this weekend it seemed right to cross the line. Getting arrested never seemed to be the right tactic at Litton (given the bombing that had been associated with those arrested). And I had always assumed I would be deported for committing any civil disobedience in the

States. However, one of the policemen has assured me that those charged for the first time will not be deported. It will be different for some of the others. Liz Walters faces up to six months in a federal penitentiary; she seems absolutely peaceful, though. About fifteen of us (women) spent a couple of hours together in the holding room after we were arrested — supposedly cooling our heels! It was actually one of the most profound conversations I have been involved in. We talked about what mattered most to us, what we thought was worth sacrificing for. We talked about the walls we had all come up against and why we couldn't be any place else.

## TRUTH TOLD WITH A TWINKLE
### (CNT, Sept. 24, 1989)

Nobody ever told me that Dan Berrigan could be fun to be with. Fascinating, yes. Fun, no.

Yet I recall the few days spent with him at a recent Faith and Resistance retreat in Mount Pleasant, Michigan, as a time of lightness and laughter. Some say it's because he's getting older; others that he's becoming freer.

He has just celebrated fifty years of being a member of the Society of Jesus. "The amazing thing is that nobody can believe it," he chuckles, "starting with myself."

He looks back on the fifty years with a sense of gratitude. "It's been magnificent — except that it's gone so quickly."

The evening was celebrated in fine style with several hundred people. "We had clowns and good food and drink and a wonderful liturgy at the end. I thought that was the best way to do it — act as though it has all been terrific — which it has."

Not that there haven't been difficulties. At one point, at the height of the protests against the Vietnam war, he was asked by his superiors to leave the United States. "There've been some close calls about my future, but that seems to be past now. I don't know if I've gotten respectable or if things have changed," he muses. "Maybe it's a little bit of both."

If he has any regret it's that it took so long for him to be awakened to social issues. "We didn't get much help in the seminary and I had to discover the real issues myself."

While others have lavished praise or heaped blame on Dan Berrigan, he himself is much more modest in his assessment of his life. "I've done something with my life, not everything, but something. You can be at peace with that kind of judgement about your life. I have a sense of the value in doing something modest—having a few friends, helping one person die well."

As he recalls the last days of one of his Jesuit brothers, one gets a sense of how Berrigan would like to die. "A certain peace radiated from him at the end, even though he had been rejected and forgotten by the Society. Something like friendship with life or reality had come to him."

Perhaps Berrigan has been reduced to modesty because of the size of the issues he has taken on—racial equality, nuclear war. "One's expectations are stopped short by life itself. You come up against a wall and you just stay there. You just dance there. You have to get rid of any sense of winning or losing, effectiveness or persuading. You just say, "I'm here because I can't be any place else.""

Throughout the retreat Berrigan kept emphasizing that resistance to militarism was primarily an act of faith rather than a question of strategy. "Our battle is not against merely human power gone wrong. It is a battle of faith, a spiritual battle against the god of death who is claiming our children. We cannot look for results or winning. It is a work of faith. Many of us see no results from this work. Are we incurably foolish or just faithful?"

However, Berrigan points out that most people in North America are blind to the depth of the struggle. "The culture prevents us from seeing clearly. We are led to see nuclear weapons as peacekeepers, abortion as an issue of women's rights, and gay people with AIDS as sinners."

Telling the truth about a culture enshrouded by lies has characterized Dan Berrigan's public life. How has he been able to speak the truth for so long – and with such a twinkle?

"I've been very fortunate in my friends, in my family, and, to a lesser degree, in my order. My friends and family have kept me relatively sane – beware of anyone who is completely sane these days!"

He has also been strengthened by frequent reference to the scriptures and the sacraments – a discipline he learned from people like Dorothy Day and Thomas Merton. "Some of us learned, in the late fifties, that unless we went back to our resources in the Bible and the sacraments, we wouldn't survive. It seems as though no matter how bad things get, these keep people going."

He stresses the importance of community. He has observed that secular communities for peace are more concerned about their political impact than about their quality of life together. "Religious communities, on the other hand, are more concerned about the quality of their life. They are not unconcerned about political action but they are not concerned about results. Strangely enough, these are the communities that have the greatest political impact."

Berrigan is under no illusion that community life is easy. "It is a difficult time for any human bonding. But there is value in whatever effort goes into keeping honesty in the air and making affection available — it all keeps chaos from the door."

His own local community (twenty Jesuits living in an apartment block in New York) has been a source of strength and encouragement for him. "We've struggled not to substitute professionalism for friendship — which is a price that has often been paid. We don't want to pay it and that's our strength as a community." Such supports for the long haul are important, he says, because there is no end in sight to the nuclear arms race.

In spite of the breathtaking moves by Gorbachev, Berrigan is convinced that changes in the American military complex are cosmetic. "Any internal disarray in the military complex is because of a slight mitigation of financial resources. There is no moral judgement that what they are doing is wrong. No hint of conversion. The worst they fear is that peace might really break out."

Berrigan's own resistance to nuclear weapons has led to many civil disobedience actions. A 1980 action at the General Electric plant in King of Prussia, Pennsylvania, has bounced around from court to court. However, it is now clear that all legal appeals have been exhausted and Dan will probably be sentenced soon. He is somewhat concerned that this will interrupt courses he is presently teaching at Loyola University in New Orleans. But not overly concerned. "I think it's a wonderful idea for a teacher to go off to jail at times. He might really believe what he's saying — which is unusual."

It is women, Berrigan emphasizes, who keep him honest about the church and about himself. "Men are bound hand and foot to property, ego, and power. They are finding it difficult to move off a dime. The women are making us move."

The situation of women in the church disturbs him greatly. "The church can't work for peace if it's being unjust to half of its members." He is often asked why he sticks with such an unjust structure. "I ask them to show me something better."

Berrigan feels he can be part of such a church as long as he is not benefiting from the injustices. "I'm probably at the edge of the church, and that allows me to be in touch with those who are coming in and going out."

In his autobiography, Berrigan sums up his life this way: "For years, he was searching for a language, an image that would contain and convey certain passionate convictions.... The light that finally flared in his soul took this form: a religious imagery of sacrifice."

When I asked him to explain his rather elliptical remark, he answered that it was a solid image but one that had to be balanced by "a humorous distance from one's own life."

Wink, wink, and twinkle.

## New Year's Day, 1990

Just when you begin to question your hope, reality answers back with a real reason for hope. We can hardly believe the marvellous news coming out of Eastern Europe. Is it possible? We have never lived in anything other than a cold-war situation. Yes, it is possible. Many toasts to peace and freedom. Ann knows some of the people involved in the changes because of her student days in Germany. She read us some letters she had received. The most poignant was from a young East German church worker who had been part of the "forum" that ignited the popular protest. "It is a happy day. Yet I watch with sadness as thousands rush madly to go shopping in West Berlin. I thought freedom was about more than shopping."

Last night we began by reading sections from W.H. Auden's Christmas oratorio, *For the Time Being*. As I

reread the oratorio some of the lines seemed to gather up
so many pieces of the year, of the years.
*Space is the Whom our lives are needed by,*
*Time is our choice of How to love and Why.*
Bill and Susan, Isabel, Jim, Mark, Luigi, and Ann—we
used to be figures with no ground. Now we are grounded
in time and space. Limited. Blessedly limited. Our lives
have been claimed and we have made our choices of how
to love and why.

CROSSING THE DIVIDE
(CNT, Feb. 18, 1990)

*Follow Me.*
These words wind their way
through the bedrock of centuries
and up through the layers
of ourselves upon selves.
When these words burst forth
upon the scene of our souls
there is a beckoning beyond
who we are and why.
There is a reckoning.
We are face to face
with Jesus, with ourselves.
In a moment, however
long or short, such a call
opens up a divide
between everything that is known
and all that remains unknown

*What Is Known*
• That there are pluses and minuses,
  debits and credits.

- That there are flowers
  springing up in our hearts
  and weeds with deep roots.
- That we sometimes say "for ever"
  and at other times say "never"
  and usually mean neither.
- That our psyche is housed
  in many rooms, empty and inhabited:
  ghosts in the basement,
  children in the bedrooms,
  visitors in the front room.
  A knock at the door may be
  an angel or a demon in disguise.
- That there are mirrors of our lives —
  some we hang up, others we take down.
- That there are conventional signs
  of when to stop and when to proceed.
- That we have baggage, vehicles, maps.
- That danger lies in the ditches
  and in the middle of the road.
- That we do our part
  so the show goes on,
  play many roles but rarely act ourselves.
- That there are rich and poor
  and we feel like neither and like both.
- That we try to do our best
  by avoiding the worst.
- That we believe within reason
  and doubt in moderation.
- That we are less than what we dream
  and more than what we think.
- That we have been here before
  and we don't know where we are.

In sum: a life.
Not perfect but predictable.

*What Is Not Known*
The Way we cannot see,
the Word we cannot speak,
the Other than ourselves.
The unaccountable, the immeasurable,
the unscripted, the unseemly,
the unseasonal.
Beyond analysis and reflection,
beyond belief.
There is only the glimpse of a face
through all the facets of our lives,
the eyes searching out
the mystery of "I",
the hands that hand
us over to ourselves and others,
the voice of the One most strange
and yet most familiar to ourselves.

*Follow Me.*
Do not wait until you are ready.
You will never be ready.
Come as you are.
And you will learn,
day to day, step by step, that
I am the Way
beyond your predictable paths
I am the Truth
beyond what you have told
I am the Life
beyond the appearance
of vitality or deadness.

And I promise you nothing
except everything
and it will cost you
not less than everything
but mean more than anything.

# About the Author

Mary Jo Leddy, a member of the Sisters of Our Lady of Sion, was the founding editor of *Catholic New Times* in 1976. She has remained involved with the newspaper in a variety of ways over the years. *Catholic New Times* is now widely recognized as a credible alternative voice in the Catholic church and has received numerous awards for journalistic excellence.

Active in peace and justice issues, Mary Jo Leddy has travelled widely in Canada and elsewhere to promote human rights. She has been a columnist for the *Toronto Star* and has commented frequently in the national media.